Staying Connected with Your Teen

Polyvagal Parenting Strategies to Reduce Reactivity, Set Limits & Build Authentic Connection

YSHAI BOUSSI, LPC

New Harbinger Publications, Inc.

Publisher's Note

NEW HARBINGER PUBLICATIONS is a registered trademark of New Harbinger Publications, Inc.

New Harbinger Publications is an employee-owned company.

Copyright © 2024 by Yshai Boussi
    New Harbinger Publications, Inc.
    5720 Shattuck Avenue
    Oakland, CA 94609
    www.newharbinger.com

All Rights Reserved

Cover design by Amy Daniel

Acquired by Ryan Buresh

Edited by Kristi Hein

Library of Congress Cataloging-in-Publication Data on file

Printed in the United States of America

26   25   24

10   9   8   7   6   5   4   3   2   1   First Printing

*To my amazing kids. You bring me so much joy,
and I'm honored to get to be your dad.*

*In loving memory of
Anne and Sam.
I still feel your love, enthusiasm, and encouragement.*

Contents

Introduction

In 2021, a national emergency in child and adolescent mental health was declared by three leading child advocacy organizations. In that same year, Surgeon General Vivek Murthy issued a warning that mental health challenges were leading to "devastating effects" among young people. The statistics are undeniable. Rates of anxiety, depression, suicide, and hospital admissions for mental health issues continue to soar.[1] As a family therapist specializing in adolescent mental health, I'm on the front lines every day with teens and families who are overwhelmed. I'm also the parent of a teen myself.

There are many plausible explanations for why adolescent mental health is such a problem right now. Accelerating climate change, gun violence, and political polarization are massive ills of our society that we've put on the laps of our teens. Social media is a megaphone that amplifies worry, fear, and unrealistic expectations for our young people. It preys on the most vulnerable among us. The technology we all love has created an expectation of instant gratification and convenience, setting up our teens to think they should always feel comfortable and be happy. Another stressor is the ever-increasing demands placed on our kids. The expectations of them, athletically and academically, are higher than ever. Add to this the fallout of a pandemic that, for many, will have a lasting negative impact that will take many years to recover from, profoundly altering the childhood of an entire generation of kids.

But perhaps the number one concern underlying all of this is an epidemic of loneliness. Our teens and young adults are increasingly feeling disconnected and alone. A 2019 survey by Signa found that 79 percent of young adults ages eighteen through twenty-two reported feeling lonely.[2] That was *before* the pandemic. Relative to millennials and boomers, Gen Z is the loneliest group. This is particularly concerning because the number one protective factor against all mental health disorders is healthy connection with others.

You may have picked up this book because you want to figure out how to have a better relationship with your teen. You may want to learn how to be more helpful or supportive when they're having a meltdown or are just shut down. Or perhaps you'd like to strike a better balance between staying connected and setting boundaries.

Feeling connected isn't a function of how many friends or loved ones we have in our life. Truly connecting with others requires a *regulated nervous system*. This is the experience of feeling grounded and settled in our body and mind. Outside this regulated state, it's very difficult to give or receive love, caring, or kindness. In fact, it's common to push away those closest to us. Under these circumstances, sometimes it can feel daunting just to reach out to someone or engage in small talk.

It's overwhelming being a parent of a teen right now. There's so much information, much of which is conflicting. For example, if connection with our teens is fundamental, then how do we connect without being a doormat? Should we be their friend? Isn't it normal for a teen to *not* want to spend time with grown-ups?

Teens are famously moody and emotionally unreliable. It's not possible to stay connected *all* the time. There will be ruptures—many, many ruptures. They will not like us very much at times. They will be mean occasionally. They won't follow through with simple requests. But we still have to stay engaged.

Our job isn't to protect our kids from the dangers and ills of our society; that's unrealistic. Instead, our job is to provide inoculation. The best way to protect our kids from the inevitable temptations, pressures, and dangerous risk-taking isn't more rules, or bigger and louder consequences; it's offering connection along with effective expectations and accountability.

This book is grounded in neuroscience and established research on adolescent development and the science of effective parenting. But perhaps most important, what I have to share with you is built on twenty-five years of experience working in the trenches with teens. I love working with teenagers. I've certainly taken my lumps in the process, but I've also learned a lot about what works and what doesn't.

Beginning as a Naïve Mentor

I began my unexpected journey of working with teenagers in 1998 as a volunteer mentor with an organization called Committed Partners for Youth (CPY) in Portland, OR. I was twenty-four, and it was an impulsive choice. My real job was using my business degree to climb the ladder as a retail executive in the buying offices of a large department store chain. Mentoring was a side gig that required a one-year commitment to spend just a couple of hours a week with an eighth grader labeled "at risk." Or so I thought.

When I signed up to be a mentor, I figured I'd simply be taking a kid to the movies or the mall once a week. Little did I know how much more would be expected of me. As mentors, we were required to attend several weekends of personal development training. Through experiential activities and vulnerable conversations, we were challenged to look at our own triggers, judgments, and biases. Some of us would get angry and defensive, others sad; some would shut down or quit. Then they sent us to the woods. We were "invited" to participate in high ropes courses with our mentees. I found myself staring down a shaky thirty-five-foot tree trunk. I told them I was afraid of heights. But this only seemed to make the facilitators more eager to get me up there. The entire way up I thought, *Why do I have to do this? And what does this have to do with helping my mentee who's way down there?* As I slowly climbed and wobbled, my body filled with anxiety and fear. My mind, with self-doubt. From below, my mentee was encouraging me! Wow, talk about humbling. The reward for getting to the top was a two-by-two-foot platform that I was expected to balance on. From there, I was "invited" to jump toward a trapeze dangling five feet away. I observed my mentee and other brave and self-conscious thirteen- and fourteen-year-olds taking on this challenge. Supporting and encouraging my mentee was easy. Taking these types of risks myself and being vulnerable was a different matter. But I did it: I jumped. I was surprised by the surge of pride I felt. Shortly afterward, during the debriefing, I got the lessons they were trying to teach. We learned that the decision to work with teens—especially those with a history of trauma, poverty, and other adversity—would be gritty work, and there might be times we'd want to quit, which was exactly what many of these kids expected and were used to. To have an impact with these kids, who were naturally distrustful and well defended, we'd have to be authentic and dependable. Perhaps most important, we'd need to have the awareness and ability to manage our own triggers as they came up.

That intense year as a mentor had a profound impact on me, and I wanted more. I discovered a passion for working with youth. That thirty-five-foot climb and five-foot jump to the trapeze became a metaphor for taking risks and going for it. At the end of that year commitment, I stayed in touch with my mentee informally for as long as I could, and I also signed up for another year with a different young person. Most significantly, I decided to quite my corporate job and take a 50-percent pay cut to work full time as a treatment counselor at the Christie School, a residential facility that housed some of the most traumatized and neglected youth in the state. I knew I had a knack for building rapport with kids, and I found myself enjoying challenging teenagers. My career path began to take shape.

I was so inspired by the youth facilitators helping us be mentors at CPY that around this same time I also chose to immerse myself in the work of facilitating intensive experiential workshops for teens. These transformative weekend intensives would welcome skeptical and shutdown kids on a Friday evening; by Sunday afternoon they'd approach a place of tears and authentic vulnerability. I had the unique opportunity to work with and learn from some brilliant facilitators. Folks like Clinton, Derrek, Hanif, and Jeremiah. While none of them had graduate degrees that I was aware of, when it came to teens and connection, they got it. They demonstrated a unique combination of thoughtfulness, kindness, and steadiness along with super-high expectations for what was possible for young people, and they had a loving way of holding them accountable when they fell short. As a facilitator, I learned the importance of personal growth and practicing what we preach with kids. If we wanted them to show up on time, we had to show up on time. If we wanted them to be vulnerable, we had to be vulnerable. If we wanted them to be silly, we would need to be silly. I learned to model patience and persistence with sayings like "out love 'em and out last 'em."

My work as a mentor, residential treatment counselor, and facilitator was often grueling and scary. I've had the privilege of seeing the light turn on in the eyes of young people whose dark history of childhood trauma I would never understand. I witnessed unreasonable resilience, strength, and heart in kids who had every reason to quit. It could also be deflating. I've been kicked, hit, spit on, and cussed out. Sometimes all by the same kid.

These raw experiences prepared me to go to graduate school and become a family therapist, the role I've had for over twenty years.

Going into graduate school, I knew I wanted to work more in depth with teenagers, but I wasn't sure about the parent and family side of things. I wasn't a parent myself, and, truth be told, I harbored some real judgment of parents. Perhaps the universe does have a way of giving us the lessons we need, as I found myself in a master's program that emphasized family therapy. I was immersed in a learning environment that strayed from individual pathology, or blaming individuals, and instead emphasized systems and context. As a result, I had an internship doing family therapy with teens. I listened to story after story of parents feeling ashamed and insecure. They were scared and sad and just wanted help. I continued my role as a family therapist during my first job at a community mental health agency. Working with parents and teens, separately and together, allowed me to help create profound change that I don't think I could have accomplished working with either group alone. My first few years as a clinician hooked me on the unmistakable benefit of collaborating with parents toward a shared goal of helping their teen. I still wasn't a parent myself, but I was pretty sure I'd be perfect at it.

And Then I Became a Parent

I recently came across this observation: "I thought I knew all there was to know about parenting until I became a parent." Boy, did that ring true for me.

Becoming a parent changed me in so many ways. My wife, Mariah, and I are the biological parents of a fifteen-year-old daughter and an eleven-year-old son. We're also foster parents to a twenty-seven-year-old who joined our family at age thirteen. I'll share more about this tough journey in the pages ahead. Parenting has been the most frustrating, humbling, rewarding, and confusing experience of my life. I sometimes catch myself daydreaming about a future as an empty nester when I might get to travel and do more of what I want. But I also settle on one fact: As stressful as it can be at times, I wouldn't trade the experience of being a parent for anything. I know I'll miss these days when they're over, so I'm trying to appreciate them now— even the ones I feel miserable about.

As a parent of a teen and tween, I feel a solidarity with you. Parenting skills and knowledge are but one important piece of an intricate puzzle that will shape our teens' behavior and how they will turn out. A lot of it is out of our hands. In my private practice I work with many parents who are accomplished therapists and psychologists in their own right, renowned members of the mental health community—even parenting experts. It's also not uncommon for me to sit across from regular parents who have figured out some things that I'm still trying to navigate with one of my own kids. I've learned from every family I've ever worked with. I'm sure I'd have something to learn from you as well.

It turns out that we're all fumbling and worried about our teens at times. But I'm certain that you're doing much more good than not. We're all doing the best we can, and hopefully always learning.

So Why This Book?

There are a lot of good books out there for parents of teens. Many of them have helped and inspired me both personally and professionally. I hope you find this one helpful in its own way.

About ten years ago, I took a training from therapist and researcher Deb Dana. She talked about *polyvagal theory*. I'm not a professor, scientist, or researcher, and typically any term that ends with the word "theory" turns me off, as I expect a dry and very cerebral, unrelatable presentation. But this was anything but that.

Understanding polyvagal theory has fundamentally changed the way I interact in the world, both personally and professionally. It's been instrumental in explaining the previously unexplainable. Grounded in the science of the autonomic nervous system, it teaches us that the way we respond to our environment begins below the surface of our awareness. In any given moment we experience some variation of three basic states: either shutdown, activated, or regulated. The state we're in has a significant influence on the way we think and act toward others and ourselves. When your teen isn't regulated, they simply cannot learn or reflect. This means anything you say will fall on deaf ears. Nor can they give or receive connection. You're bumping up against a nervous system that is stuck. To help our teens, we have to help them expand their capacity to experience a regulated nervous system.

A grounding mantra that I live by is *connection before correction*. Connection is the foundation of everything that we want for our teens and young adults. It's the root of happiness, meaning, purpose, and even longevity. But our job is also to provide correction. Teens need guidance from adults. They need expectations and accountability for those times they fall short. In fact, when approached lovingly, expectations and accountability breed trust and strengthen connection overall.

As you think about behavior—yours and your teen's—through the lens of their developing brain and nervous system, you will find yourself less reactive and more compassionate and thoughtful. The relationship between the two of you will improve.

This book is not chiefly about better parenting skills, although I have plenty of concrete tips. My assumption is that you actually have a lot of skills. Believe it or not, your teen does too. In many cases, the problems we're having with our teens are due not to a lack of skills, but rather to our inability to access the skills we have.

This book is divided into three parts. Part 1 will give you vital information that helps explain why your teen acts the way they do. It's a look behind the curtain. Chapter 1 will talk about the extended period of adolescence and what it means for your child, what you can expect at different stages, and how to be helpful at each one. Chapter 2 is a brief primer on the developing adolescent brain, zeroing in on three essential components: the prefrontal cortex, the amygdala, and dopamine. You'll come away understanding why your teen can be at once brilliant, moody, and impulsive. Chapter 3 will be your intro to polyvagal theory. More specifically, this chapter will explain why your teen is often either shut down or activated and how to help shape their nervous system so that they can experience more calm and regulated energy.

Part 2 zeroes in on connection. Chapter 4 will give you some concrete skills to help you experience more connection with your teen. In chapter 5, you'll learn about the attitude and mindset required for creating sustainable and authentic connection with your teen. Chapter 6 offers insights into peer relationships, along with tools to help you facilitate more healthy connections among your teen and their peers. Chapter 7 is about your teen's relationships with other adults, an essential aspect of helping them feel less alone and more connected to their community, not to mention an important way for you to gain some much-needed breaks.

Part 3 addresses expectations and accountability. Chapter 8 will teach you a framework for providing effective expectations. Chapter 9 presents an updated understanding of accountability, along with a guide for effective responses when those expectations aren't met. There will be stories throughout, with circumstances, names, and details that represent composites of actual clients.

I've had a lot of roles with teenagers over the years—mentor, experiential facilitator, residential counselor, therapist, foster parent, and parent. But if I could distill all I've learned into one lesson, it would be this: We're all doing the best we can, and when we know better, we do better. Willingness to learn and adapt to the ever-changing circumstances, needs, and personality of our teens is essential for this journey. While you surely have made mistakes, you aren't failing your teen, and their struggles aren't your fault. You're not a bad parent, and you don't have a bad kid. But you're reading this book because there's a teen or preteen in your life whom you adore, and you want to do your best by them. While you may never work with me as a client, I hope you feel my support and guidance in these pages. Whatever you're going through right now with your teen, know that you are anything but alone. We're in this together.

Let's get started!

PART I

Teenagers: A Look Behind the Curtain

As promised in the introduction, this first part of the book offers essential information to help you understand why your teen acts the way they do. As we look behind the curtain into what's going on in their developing brain, baffling behaviors should start to make more sense. In chapter 1, we focus on the extended period of adolescence. Armed with this knowledge, you'll be better prepared for what to expect in different stages. Rather than throwing up your hands in despair—or sternly laying down the law, when they really weren't capable of making a reasoned choice about taking risks and avoiding consequences—you'll find helpful, practical strategies for handling each stage more effectively.

In chapter 2, we get to know the developing adolescent brain. You'll start to become familiar with the prefrontal cortex, the amygdala, and dopamine, and how their workings lead to those teen impulses, behaviors, and frustrating responses to your well-meaning efforts. And even if you've never heard of polyvagal theory, I promise you'll start to recognize how it applies to your teen (to every human, really) as you read chapter 3. It's empowering to finally understand why your teen is often either shut down or activated, and to know how to be a reliable ally in their ups and downs with their developing nervous system. With your help, they can start to experience more periods of calm and regulated energy and can better handle the challenges—and enjoy the rewards—of their teen years.

CHAPTER 1

Adolescence: A Transition That Keeps Going, and Going, and...

What do a fruit fly and your teen have in common? Yes, they're both diffi-cult to control and stubborn at times. But the other thing they have in common is that they both experience an adolescence. In fact, adolescence is such a normal aspect of development that we actually share it with most other species.

Adolescence is an essential transition period from childhood to mature adulthood.

Mammals, reptiles, and even insects experience an adolescence. The length of this transition varies, but its key feature is developing the ability to think and act like a mature member of the group. This happens primarily through experience over time.

We all want our kids to ultimately think, act, and feel like a mature member of our group. That's what the journey of parenting during this period is all about. The good news is that, in the twenty-first century, ado-lescence happens over a very long time period. The bad news is that adoles-cence happens over a very long time period.

Adolescence starts biologically when kids reach puberty, a pretty clear marker that's been starting earlier and earlier. When it ends is a bit murkier. After all, how do we define "mature adult"? Is it eighteen? Twenty-one? We need some way to measure this stage, if for no other reason than to affirm when a teen has made it to adulthood.

The purpose of adolescence is to get teens ready to enter adulthood and be successful at it. Given this critical task, we parents need to clarify—and in most cases, redefine—what that means in today's complex and fast-changing world.

What Is Successful Adulthood?

When I was growing up, the implicit and explicit messages I received from my parents about being a successful adult hinged on going to college, making a lot of money, marrying a "nice Jewish girl," and having kids. (Although to this day, their guiding principle is "just be happy.")

Their hopes and dreams for me made sense, given their own childhood histories, the era they were parenting in, and the information they had at the time.

Today, we as parents have a lot more information—perhaps too much. It would have been impossible to write a book like this three decades ago. Indisputably, one key thing we've learned over the last few decades is that adolescence is a critical time of learning that will fundamentally shape the trajectory of the adulthood that follows.

Historically, the common markers signifying the full entry into adulthood are career, marriage or long-term relationship, financial independence, and kids. These markers were once typically met by the early to mid twenties. Now, in America, it's closer to thirty or even later for some. Of course, it's now very common, even typical, to reach full adulthood without getting married or having children. So we need to keep looking at what makes us an adult. Perhaps even more importantly, how we can reach these milestones in healthy and fulfilling ways.

You and I are swimming upstream against a culture that wants our kids to find happiness in consumption and external aesthetics at the expense of internal depth and kindness. Technology, along with its countless benefits to society, is also eroding their capacity to focus, delay gratification, empathize, and connect in authentic ways. It turns out that just wanting our kids to be happy is not only unrealistic but also a recipe for disappointment and fragility.

This is why parenting becomes a lot easier when we are clear about what values and skills we want our kids to grow up with. If you're like our family, you want your child to become an adult who is kind, works hard, cares about others and the world, has fulfilling relationships, and is resilient.

But if your family is anything like ours, your kids often seem to go out of their way while at home to prove that they have none of these values or skills. It often takes input from other parents, teachers, and coaches to remind us that we actually are more on track than we think.

When your values are clear, parenting an adolescent can be about helping your kids develop and internalize skills that will set them up for success as adults. This is a process with stages, for sure; however, it's anything but linear. Your child will absolutely gain more skills and maturity over time. They will become more self-regulated, empathetic, socially skilled, ethical, and cognitively mature. But these will all happen on an uneven timeline, and there will be backsliding.

Adolescence is like a slow cooker (a very slow cooker). The core ingredients are in there. What we add or leave out, and when, will go a long way toward determining how this meal turns out. It's such a long period that it can be helpful to break it down into three stages. Since each stage comes with its own unique challenges and opportunities, understanding where your adolescent is at will help guide your decision making and expectations.

The Three Stages of Adolescence

If puberty starts at age eleven to twelve, on average, and mature adulthood arrives around thirty, that's (gulp) a long time in adolescence. Breathe!

We'll get through this. Jokes aside, this prolonged period of adolescence is a good thing. It allows our teens and young adults more time to define their values, learn from their mistakes and successes, and identify a lifestyle that will work best for them over the next fifty-plus years of their life.

For parents, it can be encouraging to know that your teen has many more meaningful years to grow and develop. Whether your child is thirteen or twenty-five, you will continue to be an extremely important person for them to lean on. Your influence and role will change, but your child will continue to seek you out as a home base of love and support on their journey.

The stages and ages I discuss here are intended only as guidelines and averages. Kids move through these stages at different paces. Some kids start puberty at age nine and move through the first phase by age twelve or thirteen. Others are late bloomers. Kids who experienced early childhood trauma and/or neglect typically go through these phases much more slowly.

Phase 1: "What Happened to My Sweet Little Boy?" (eleven through fourteen)

Mike was a super cuddly toddler and oh so sweet. In elementary school, he loved wrestling with his dad, the Cars movies, and Captain Underpants and Dogman graphic novels. At his worst, he would have a meltdown, throw himself on the floor, and call his mom or dad a poop head.

Now he's thirteen. The cute, squeaky high voice has vanished. And the avoidance of showers is noteworthy. But these are the predictable and easy things to deal with. Much more difficult is Mike's separation. He's replaced cuddling with physical distance, as though a new virus that only he knows about has engulfed the family. The language? Certainly not poop head and rarely involving full sentences. And the arguing. He's tireless. The dad jokes that were once met with glee are now met with crickets or disdain. His parents appear to have gone from hero to zero.

This period starts at around eleven and ends at around fourteen. This is typically the most turbulent time for kids and parents. This phase is defined by a lot of emotional intensity (both highs and lows) and arguing. It's often really hard on parents and marriages. If you're having a hard time personally, you're not alone. Adolescents, often the firstborn in particular, have a way of turning cracks into chasms.

Laurence Steinberg is a professor of psychology at Temple University and a leading researcher on adolescence. In his 1994 book *Crossing Paths*, he chronicled a longitudinal study of over two hundred families. Fifty percent of the mothers and nearly a third of the fathers in the sample reported suffering a decline in mental health once their firstborn entered adolescence. They reported experiences of low self-worth, feelings of rejection, and physical symptoms of distress, like headaches, stomachaches, and insomnia.

Steinberg wrote: "We are much better able to predict what an adult was going through psychologically by looking at his or her child's development than by knowing the adult's age."[3]

Phase 1 for adolescents involves great emotional intensity and a limited capacity to slow it down, like a race car with no brakes. They're gonna go really fast and crash a lot! But they do start to find their brakes more in the next phase.

Five Tips to Support Your Phase 1 Kid

- *Don't take their outbursts personally.* Your phase 1 kid is particularly impulsive. Not just behaviorally, but emotionally as well. Their emotions come on with force and speed. They will be very hard on you at times, even mean. Your young adolescent will need you to give them grace in these moments. Sometimes they'll need a do-over or just a few minutes to regroup.

- *Expect extreme, all-or-nothing thinking.* You will likely find your teen expressing extreme views. They'll either love or hate many things—no in between. They will often use terms like "everyone," "no one," "never," and "always." They may seem ecstatic and then miserable.

- *Expect to be challenged.* The phase 1 teen's prefrontal cortex is starting to come online, which means they're thinking and reasoning much better than they did a few years ago. But since they don't have the emotional brake system yet, they will often be extra argumentative while struggling to find an off-ramp. They may also call out their parents. In many cases, they will have a valid point, and we need to respond with humility and acknowledge our missteps.

- *Minimize social media time.* The impact social media has on teens overall is more complex than popular commentary typically indicates. There truly are pros and cons, and it affects different kids in different ways. However, there is some research that is more clear. Younger adolescents are more susceptible than older teens to the negative effects of social media. In a perfect world, these younger adolescents would not have access to social media.

- *Provide supervision and monitoring.* Your young adolescent will gradually handle more autonomy and independence, but it's not time to let go of the rope. They might think they're ready for it, and they may ask for a ton of freedom and privacy. Consider what level of freedom and autonomy your individual child is ready for. This should be based on what their behavior is showing you, not solely on what they say they want, and definitely not based on what their friends get to do, which from their perspective is usually way better than what they're stuck with.

Phase 2: "I Thought We Were Over This!?" (fifteen through seventeen)

Mike's sixteen now. The arguing has decreased a lot. He's much more reasonable. He's got a lot more freedom now. He's getting decent grades. Whew! Good to see him so independent. One day, during your routine trip to the bedroom to grab his rotting clothes off the floor, out of the corner of your eye you spot something lying on his bed. Is that basil and oregano? Hmm, didn't know he was interested in herbs and the culinary arts. What's that unique pen next to it? Is it a stylus for his iPad? Is that an external thumb drive that he uses to save his work for school? Nope, it's weed and weirdly high-tech vaping equipment.

The nice thing about Mike at this stage is that when confronted about the drugs, he's able to hear his parents out. He also makes some valid points. He tells his parents, "I'm getting decent grades, and I'm usually home on time, and I have a job." He then twists his parents' judgment into a pretzel by asserting that so many kids smoke weed, and he doesn't do it very often. Of course, he also tells them he was holding most of it for a friend.

In Mike's mind, he really is doing pretty well, but he recognizes that he probably smokes weed a little too often. All his parents can think about is What else don't we know about his secret world? Is he doing coke on a mirror coffee table? Is he going to descend into a life of drugs, poverty, and regret? Will he struggle like his older cousin? Worry and panic start to set in. His parents find themselves lecturing Mike about the importance of college and his future. A diatribe he's all too familiar with.

Fortunately, Mike and his parents were able to have a thoughtful and honest conversation about what was going on. His parents were able to temporarily put their anxiety and fear about his future to rest, calm down, and focus on concern for Mike and curiosity about his experience. Seeing his parents calm and genuinely concerned, Mike's defenses were settled, and he opened up about his struggle with anxiety and why he was trying to deal with it on his own so as not to worry his parents. While he didn't promise that he would never smoke weed again, he did agree to keep it out of the house, limit it, and see a therapist.

Phase 2 occurs around ages fifteen through seventeen. During this period, adolescents start to put pieces of the puzzle together, and the intensity of their emotions begins leveling off. In fact, by the age of sixteen, adolescents score just as high on cognitive tests as they ever will. This means that, from a purely intellectual perspective, they're as capable as we are—and as they'll ever be. So the question then becomes, "Shouldn't they be able to go to graduate school, work a demanding job, or function as adults?"

The answer is yes, as long as they're well rested, not stressed, not in a hurry, and not dealing with any other adversity. Once you introduce stress, sleep deprivation, or another challenge to adolescents, these cognitive skills fall off a cliff compared to how an adult would be affected. Many of us underestimate our kids' intelligence and understanding—but overestimate their capacity for self-control and stress management.

While teens during this period are still operating with the intensity of a race car, they're starting to figure out their brake system and aren't crashing as much. You should be noticing more impulse control relative to phase 1. But be prepared. Just when you get comfortable and lie back with your hands behind your head, like "I got this this"...crash! Your child makes a poor decision with complicated results, and you find yourself feeling the stress of years past and a developmental stage you thought you were over.

These moments humble us; they are reminders that our kids are still very much squarely in adolescence.

Five Tips to Support Your Phase 2 Kid

- *Focus on influence, not control.* The more you leaned on control and monitoring during elementary school and their early adolescence, the harder this phase will be for you and your teen. Having influence with your teen means you build and strengthen a relationship that's based on mutual respect and understanding. It requires listening and being influenced by your teen's ideas and perspectives. Having influence means your teen cares about your opinions and follows your requests because they respect you and care about their relationship with you.

- *Spend quality family and one-on-one time.* I'll spend much more time talking about this in the next section, but know that your teen still needs quality time as a family and individual, distraction-free time with you. This can't be overstated. The better the relationship your teen has with you, the better judgment they'll show when it comes to friends, dating, drugs, alcohol, and other risky behaviors online and off.

- *Value their intelligence.* Your teen has a lot of intelligence and capacity to think things through. When they're calm and grounded, listen to them and take them seriously. This will not only increase your influence but also help you be a better parent, because they'll often share insights and points of view that you hadn't considered. In fact, many developmental psychologists who study adolescents feel that we should lower the voting age to sixteen for this very reason.

- *Collaborate as much as possible.* Phase 2 teens need to feel like they have a seat at the table of decision making. Whenever possible, when you're making decisions about rules, expectations, moves, family trips, or anything else that calls for a choice, elicit their input. You have the final say, but do your best to factor in their thoughts and feelings.

- *Give them the why.* Teens have a really hard time with being told no "because I said so." Or "because I'm the parent." This is extremely frustrating. Any no's you offer should be grounded in issues of safety or your values. For example, wanting them to be home by midnight on Halloween may be because they need a decent night's sleep for school the next day. You want them to have device-free time at night or during the day because you value single-focused attention, quality family time, or the benefits of activities that don't involve devices (which typically require more delayed gratification and patience). Chores are often about contributing to the family community and being helpful.

Phase 3: "What Do You Mean, They Might Not Be Ready Until Thirty!?" (eighteen and up)

Mike's now twenty-three and just graduated from college. He's got a good relationship with his parents and is able to appreciate their support and love. He looks back on his early adolescence and acknowledges that he was a handful at times.

Mike is living at home and has a full-time job. But he's feeling lost. He's torn between the messages he's received about finding a career that's lucrative and the messages about pursuing work that he loves, which he hasn't figured out yet. Should he be enjoying his youth and having fun with friends, or buckling down and focusing on his future? For the first time in his life, he doesn't have the structure and seasons of school to anchor him. He's dating someone cool, but he panics at the thought of being with them forever. Plus, both he and his parents are trying to navigate the new boundaries and roles of an adult child living with their parents.

This period is roughly age eighteen and up—sometimes way up, as I've mentioned. Phase 3 is about becoming a better driver behind the wheel. In this book, I primarily address phases 1 and 2, but I'll share more about phase 3 in the epilogue.

CHAPTER 2

The Brain: A Lot Is Happening in That Thick Skull of Theirs

The knock on the door came at 3 a.m. Startled and groggy, Lisa opened the door and found her daughter, Brianna, standing beside a police officer. Lisa was stunned, her mind racing. She thought Brianna was upstairs sleeping. The officer told her that Brianna and several friends had hopped the fence of a private pool, gone skinny dipping, and gotten drunk on beer and hard seltzer. The officer said that charges could be pressed for trespassing and Brianna's being a minor in possession of alcohol.

He was firm. Brianna was horrified and embarrassed. Lisa was in shock.

Then the officer's stern tone dropped to one of compassion. He said that if Brianna would commit to therapy and doing some volunteer work in the community, he might be able to convince the family whose pool they were in to not press charges. Brianna agreed.

When I met Brianna for our first session, I was impressed at how articulate and thoughtful she was. She was brilliant. She had a 3.9 GPA and, although she was only a freshman, was on her varsity volleyball team. Her stats certainly didn't fit with the type of kid that would do this sort of thing.

I was really curious about the mismatch I observed between how she appeared—not only in my office but also at school and in the community—and this insanely dumb choice to so brazenly sneak into a random private pool.

I asked her why she thought she'd done what she did. She had no idea, other than that it seemed fun in the moment.

Before my meeting with Brianna, I'd met with her parents, Lisa and Damon. They exhibited all the appropriate emotions any of us would have had in that situation: worried, sad, angry, embarrassed, and confused. They wanted to know what kind of punishment was appropriate. But they were loving and involved parents. There were no red flags in this family that would explain such a lack of judgment on the part of an incredibly intelligent and sweet kid.

My third meeting was a session with Brianna and her parents together. I conveyed some important perspectives: "Brianna isn't a bad kid. She's also not a perfect kid. Staying loving and connected to her in this situation is paramount. Accountability is also important. A heartfelt in-person apology to the owners of the property, combined with doing something helpful and kind for them, and participating in therapy, are fantastic opportunities to build back trust and turn this into a learning opportunity."

I went on to explain a lot of what I thought was going on. I was as clear with them as I will be with you. It's important to note that explaining is not the same as excusing. So I talked about the adolescent brain: how it is uniquely built to take risks, how susceptible it is to losing impulse control, particularly when peers are involved. These types of lapses in judgment are unrelated to intelligence or even character. As I will soon share with you, I talked to them about the prefrontal cortex, dopamine, and the amygdala. We therapists refer to this as psychoeducation. *This type of information can be very helpful to both parents and teens.*

As Lisa and Damon took in this deeper understanding of what was happening in Brianna's brain, it was easy to see their bodies settle down and regulate. This information helped them not take Brianna's behavior so personally or feel like they were bad parents. As for my work with Brianna, by learning more about her brain and her unique temperament—which included an above-average penchant for risk-taking—I could help set her up to be in a better position to think before she acted in the future. Even better, Brianna and her parents were able to talk about what happened from a place of curiosity and learning together. Ironically, they grew closer and more trusting as a family than ever before—an outcome that is not uncommon.

This chapter will provide you with an extended version of that same information I offered Brianna and her parents. Just as Brianna did, I think your teen will find this interesting and helpful as well.

The most significant and interesting aspect of adolescence—and the most hopeful, in terms of understanding and helping both parents and teens navigate these years—has to do with the brain. Not the whole brain, but a few specific components: the prefrontal cortex (PFC), the amygdala, and the neurotransmitter dopamine. In feedback from thousands of parents over the years, I have heard over and over again that learning about these three things has been one of the most helpful steps in understanding their adolescent.

The Prefrontal Cortex

The human brain is full size by age ten, often earlier. But it's only 80 percent mature. The 20 percent that's still evolving is in the prefrontal cortex, the region behind the forehead (from here on we'll call it the PFC). This part of the brain is responsible for advanced skills like planning ahead, impulse control, and regulating emotions. During adolescence, the PFC isn't growing—it's being remodeled, or shaped, by a process called *synaptic pruning.*

Synapses are the way connections are made in our brains, allowing us to learn. We're born with an abundance of immature synapses. The ones we need most during early childhood are the ones that mature first; for example, those associated with walking, talking, fine motor skills, and bonding. Think of synapses as branches and leaves on a tree. During childhood, that tree is growing rapidly. Once adolescence arrives, that tree is full grown. The adolescent brain has an abundance of fully mature synapses in the PFC. This period is no longer about growing new branches and leaves (synapses); rather, it's about shaping what's there. Synaptic pruning is a "use it or lose it" process. The synaptic connections we use get stronger; the ones we ignore get frail and eventually die off. This is also referred to as *plasticity* or *malleability*—our brain's ability to learn in response to experience.

A house analogy can be helpful. My wife, Mariah, and I bought our first house together shortly before we married. It was a classic starter house that needed lots of work, and we loved it. It was built in 1905, was 900 square feet, and sat on a full-size, 50-by-100-foot lot near the neighborhood Mariah grew up in. We lived in that house for five years and put a lot of sweat equity into it. We refinished the beautiful oak floors, put tiling in the bathroom and kitchen, and painted to improve and beautify the house that had so much character.

We moved out after five years, when our daughter was two and a half. We planned to expand our family to include our foster son, who was thirteen, and another child we hoped to have soon.

It's been fifteen years since that move, and we occasionally walk by that house. From the outside, it's clear that the current occupants have further enhanced the space surrounding the house. The diversity of native plants, shrubs, and flowers is a significant upgrade from the dandelion-filled yard that we'd left.

What's worth noting is that the fundamental structure of this house hasn't changed a bit since 1905. It has the same brick foundation, the same layout, and the same square footage (with the exception of one added bathroom). The studs and foundation are exactly the same as they were in the original build.

So what does this have to do with your adolescent's brain? The changes happening to your adolescent's PFC are the equivalent of what was happening to our house in 1905. The blueprints are being drawn, the design is being determined, and soon the foundation will be set and the concrete poured. By a person's mid twenties, the house is built. The rest of life is about updating and improving on it.

The adolescent period of learning in specific and foundational ways is an exciting window of opportunity for every growing individual. But learning and specializing cuts both ways, allowing us to acquire both healthy and unhealthy skills.

Steinberg writes: "Plasticity opens the brain's windows to the outside world, but open windows can let in pollen, noise, and mosquitoes just as easily as ocean breezes, birds, and the fragrances of flowers."[4]

Some of the beautiful skills and habits that our adolescents are learning during this construction may include empathy, music, self-discipline, foreign languages, resilience, social skills, wilderness survival, and antiracism. On the other hand, this construction may be getting built in a way that forms negative habits and traits, such as intolerance, impulsivity, social isolation, or addiction.

It's often a combination of all of these. This book aims to help you build up more of your teen's positive skills and attributes by helping them shape their PFC and nervous system in positive ways.

They Learn Faster

The adolescent PFC is primed not just to learn, but also to learn quickly and efficiently, thanks to myelin. Myelin is like the rubber that encases an electrical cord. It protects the nerve cells and enables much faster connections between neurons in the brain and nervous system. The myelination in the PFC is what makes learning much more efficient for adolescents.

In his viral *Smarter Every Day* video episode, "The Backwards Brain Bicycle,"[5] Destin Sandlin demonstrates brain plasticity beautifully. He has his bike reverse engineered so that when the handle bars are turned left, the front wheel turns right, and when they're turned right, it goes left. He documents how it took him eight months to learn how to ride the bike this way. As a public speaker, he takes this bike with him on stages and offers people $200 to ride the bike about ten feet, and it appears that no one is able to make it to collect their money. Here's the kicker: Toward the end of the video, he asks his son, who's about six, to try it out. It takes the six-year-old just three weeks to learn.

Kids and adolescents are able to learn faster.

The amount and degree of changes happening in your adolescent's PFC is great news. No matter how much your child might be struggling, there's plenty of time and lots of opportunity for them to learn and change in fundamental and positive ways.

We parents need to help our adolescents develop a healthy, mature PFC so they can better manage their emotions, improve their judgment, and think before they act. But it's not all on us. We can only keep doing the best we can by continuing to learn and adapt through the adolescent years. We need community, support, and some luck. Oh, and a helpful and timely book is always a good idea, especially when you're up against your teenager's amygdala.

The Amygdala

Has your child ever gotten angry or overly emotional for no apparent reason? Don't laugh. As I described in chapter 1, young adolescents in phase 1, in particular, experience their lives in primarily emotional ways—largely because of their amygdala.

The amygdala is in the lower and older part of the brain called the *limbic system*. And humans didn't evolve with an amygdala for the sole purpose of being mean to their parents. There's a better explanation.

The amygdala is like the smoke detector in our brain. It's necessary and important and designed to save our life. In the event of a life-threatening emergency, our amygdala will help us live another day by communicating with our nervous system (more on this in the next chapter), enabling us to fight, flee, or freeze.

Unfortunately, for so many of our kids, their smoke detector is, in effect, being triggered by burning toast. These false alarms nevertheless feel very real in their body.

When any of us lose our cool, we're experiencing an amygdala hijack. Anger or rage masks the deep fear and takes over, and we lose it. We've all been there and done that, and it can leave us full of shame.

Experiencing an amygdala hijack doesn't always look like aggression. In my case, when in this state, I'm more likely to shut down and withdraw (flee) than to yell. The difference is the degree to which we externalize or internalize. A lot of this is built into our temperaments. My son is more of an externalizer when his amygdala takes over, whereas my daughter is more of an internalizer. Like me, she's more likely to get quiet and flee. Our son is more like his mother in this regard.

Teens who externalize their feelings command a lot more attention than the ones who internalize. But just because your child is quiet and not drawing attention to themself doesn't mean that they're not also spending a lot of time hijacked by their amygdala. These kids are just doing more freezing and fleeing. The quiet ones need our attention and care too.

An interesting study asked children and adults of ages ranging from eight to thirty-two to look at a series of pictures of frightened faces as their brains were scanned with fMRI, which monitors brain activity. Relative to the children or adults, adolescents had a stronger amygdala response to the pictures.[6] The implication is that, under the best of circumstances, adolescents are more likely to experience fearful and emotional reactions. When you factor in early trauma or neglect, the differences become extreme.

The PFC is our first line of protection against activating our amygdala. When it's working, it sifts through information and experiences before determining whether to send it to the amygdala. Since adolescents' PFC isn't fully developed yet, for many of them stressful experiences—what would otherwise be mild stressors, such as a homework assignment, chore, losing a game, or conflict with a peer—go straight through to their amygdala. Thus they often respond disproportionately with an angry outburst, shutting down, or storming off. And it can happen quickly.

Be aware that your teen's activated amygdala will often trigger your amygdala. You can easily become two rams locking horns. In these moments, it's crucial that you access your PFC. This might require taking a time-out, taking some slow deep breaths, or using other coping skills. It's not fair to expect our kids to do this as quickly or efficiently as we can. As adults with more developed brains, we need to hold ourselves to a higher standard. However long it takes you to redirect to your PFC, it will take your teen that much longer.

Don't take their amygdala hijacks personally; they can't help it. These outbursts are a hard but normal part of adolescence, particularly early adolescence. Remember, we're trying to explain, not excuse, their behavior. We'll talk about accountability in chapter 9.

Dopamine

A third aspect of the adolescent brain that functions in a way particular to this life transition has to do with *dopamine*, a neurotransmitter in our reward system. It's what gives us that experience of joy or excitement in anticipation of things—anticipating the next episode of your favorite binge-worthy show, getting together with a great friend, or that transcendent experience in nature. For me, it might be sinking my spoon into Tillamook Monster

Cookie ice cream, playing a board game with friends and family, floating across a lake on my paddle board, or playing basketball.

Adolescents release much more dopamine in response to experiences than children or adults do. What's good for us is great for them! They just have more fun than we do. Some days, this doesn't seem fair, and I envy the amount of joy my daughter gets out of her time with friends or talking about her latest passion. Okay, I'm kidding about the envy part, but it's good to appreciate this aspect of adolescence. It's a fun and exciting time in so many ways.

The flip side, of course, is that being easily drawn to exciting and novel experiences, combined with an unreliable PFC, is a recipe for dumb and regrettable decisions. Recall the story of Brianna that opened this chapter.

By the time teens reach sixteen, during phase 2 of adolescence, they have the same capacity to learn and understand that we do. They don't make bad decisions because of a lack of knowledge or smarts. Ask most teens whether they understand the dangers of drinking and driving or distracted driving. Check. The importance of trust? Check. The importance of doing well in school and "trying their best"? Check. Check. Check. Check. In most cases, our kids get it. So what's the problem?

It comes down to this combination of an immature PFC with a flood of dopamine. Psychologists use the term *hyperrational thinking* to describe the way adolescents typically overestimate the rewards of an activity while downplaying the costs.

Brianna respects her parents and doesn't want to lose their trust. She knows how important sleep is to her mental health, and that if she were to sneak out she'd end up feeling guilty and extra tired the next day. She's also aware that there's a reasonable chance that she'd get caught, and it would break trust with her parents. But it's 11, she's feeling lonely and bored, and she just got a text from a friend inviting her to meet up at the park. Though she's well aware of the many and clear reasons to stay home, the dopamine flood she gets from the anticipated excitement of sneaking out late and seeing some friends is already improving her mood. So the decision to go out wins.

It's important to note here that this isn't a personal slight against her parents. It's not about them at all.

The combination of an immature PFC and a rush of dopamine will make your teen more likely to take risks or make impulsive decisions. Add peers to the mix, and risk-taking increases even further. This is neither good nor bad; it's just part of the deal. Our job is to help teens find healthy and creative outlets for safe risk-taking.

So there's a lot happening in those developing brains. I hope at this point it makes more sense to you why they can feel so easily overwhelmed and out of control. They know it, too, and it doesn't make sense to them either. It's hard for them and for us at times. But it can also be an exciting and thrilling time (for them).

Remember the ways that you were similarly obsessed or impulsive or did silly or dumb things when you were their age? Your child's PFC will mature just as yours did. They'll look back, just as you do now, and wonder aloud, "What was I thinking?" You'll be able to tell them, "Actually, you weren't."

CHAPTER 3

Their Nervous System: Why It Feels Like You Yelled (Even If You Didn't)

I was leaning against our kitchen counter, arms folded. I was tense. At the moment our house was quiet and calm, even peaceful. I looked up at the clock: It was a quarter till 4. I needed to give James the fifteen-minute warning to prepare him to end his video game time.

James is our foster son; he was fourteen at the time. I've never met a kid with a bigger heart or a kinder soul. Mariah met James when he was five while working at a children's treatment center, and she had mentored him since he was seven. After James had spent more than a decade of bouncing around different foster homes, including one that was extremely abusive, the three of us decided that we were ready and able to have him join our family full time. When the Department of Human Services (DHS) announced this placement officially, James said it was one of the happiest days of his life. We were excited as well. We loved him and already considered him one of our kids and an integral part of our family. While Mariah and I both had extensive experience working with behaviorally and emotionally challenged kids, we felt a mixture of excitement and anxiety. We knew this was probably the hardest thing we would ever do. Still, we felt we had the skills to help James heal and become a full part of our family.

Neither of us anticipated just how hard it would be to help a teenager heal from a lifetime of trauma.

James was intelligent. He knew what he wanted and how he wanted to behave. He genuinely wanted to do well with us. But his nervous system—with its fourteen years of stored trauma, neglect, and insecure attachment—told a different story. His nervous system anticipated danger at every corner. He experienced any type of limit as a threat. When he wasn't activated, angry, or on edge, he was disconnected and difficult to reach. Finding moments of regulation, calm, and peace with him was difficult, if not impossible.

I went down to give James his fifteen-minute warning. He said "Okay," but I couldn't tell if he'd actually taken in what I'd said. At 3:59, I was back in the kitchen, preparing to tell him his time was up. I was anxious and dysregulated myself. I thought about ignoring the expectation. We both would have loved another hour of peace and avoidance. But James required clear and consistent expectations. I needed to follow through on the 4 p.m. end time. But I was scared. There was a chance he'd get off the game, no problem—and also a chance that he'd blow up and become aggressive.

I swallowed my fear and went down to tell him that it was time to turn off his PlayStation. He abruptly replied, "Hold on!" The anger in his voice let me know that this might be one of those times when this doesn't go well.

I left the room to give him some space, lingering around the corner, hoping, praying that he would turn it off and I wouldn't have to go back in there. My heart was racing.

Five, then ten minutes later, I knew I had to go back in there. My voice was more firm and louder this time, which only escalated him further. I told him that he needed to get off now or he would lose time the next day. This set him off, yelling and swearing. He stood up and punched the screen three times as hard as he could. He stormed out of the room. I knew better than to follow him.

James did eventually settle. We were able to talk about what had happened, sort of. But it didn't last. Sadly, despite the three of us putting all our energy into James's healing process, his unsafe behavior continually escalated. We all, James included, did our best, but we weren't able to give him the support he needed to live safely in our home.

We continued to remain actively involved in James's life, helping him get through high school, maintaining frequent family visits, and participating in family therapy with him.

What finally worked was having James live in a group home, with frequent home visits where we could practice coregulation, coping skills, and problem solving. Very slowly—over time, and with the help of many skilled therapists, social workers, and other foster parents—we all learned how to recognize each other's emotional states, when our nervous systems were activated, and how to support each other through that process. It's not always perfect, but it's a huge improvement on where we started so many years ago.

James is now twenty-seven and doing well. We're super proud of him because he's worked hard and made a lot of progress. He still apologizes to us for how he acted. But the truth is, it wasn't his fault. He never wanted his time with us to go down that way, but his adolescent nervous system—not his thoughts, desires, or wishes—ruled the day.

The funny thing about parenting is that no matter how much you know or how skilled you think you are, as time goes by, there's always a sense of *if only I'd known then what I know now.*

Enter Polyvagal Theory

What follows will get a bit technical, but I promise to keep it short. Our autonomic nervous system has two branches: the sympathetic and the parasympathetic. The sympathetic system, which begins in the middle of the spinal cord, is our fight-or-flight system. The parasympathetic includes an important nerve called the *vagus*. The vagus nerve has two pathways. One pathway, the *dorsal vagal*, extends from the brainstem down the spinal cord, connecting the lungs, heart, and diaphragm. The other pathway, the *ventral vagal*, also descends but then extends back up and connects to the neck, throat, eyes, and ears.

Researcher Stephen Porges discovered and developed groundbreaking insights into how the autonomic nervous system affects our reality.[7] He zeroed in on the vagus nerve and called his insights *polyvagal theory* (PT). Countless therapists, myself included, apply this theory to help people heal. As brilliant as Porges's insights were, it was one of his colleagues, Deb Dana, who helped the rest of us make sense of this science in a practical way. Dana is a clinician and consultant who has authored numerous books about polyvagal theory.[8] PT isn't a technique or protocol, but a framework and way of thinking about ourselves in relation to others. The three principles of PT are the hierarchy of states, neuroception, and coregulation. Behind these fancy words are simple concepts that I'll try to describe in lay terms.

Principle 1: The Three-State Hierarchy of Our Nervous System

The sympathetic nervous system, along with those two branches of the vagus nerve—dorsal (on the bottom) and ventral (on top)—comprise the three states that have enabled humans to survive for hundreds of millions of years. The oldest system is dorsal vagal, or what I often refer to as "shutdown." The next state is the sympathetic, or what I often refer to as "activated." Finally, the most evolved state is *ventral vagal*, or what I refer to as "regulated." Regardless of what you call each state, you know it when you're in it—as you'll see.

Dana offers a ladder metaphor to help us understand this hierarchy of different states. As you read about each state, remember that a healthy nervous system is a flexible nervous system. We're expected to move through these states. Problems occur only when we get stuck on the middle and lower rungs of the ladder. At the same time, no one is permanently in a regulated state either, and it's a fool's errand to chase it.

THE SHUTDOWN STATE

This is the least evolved state—and the bottom rungs of the ladder is a hard place to be. From an evolutionary perspective, this state offered us the chance for survival by attempting to hide or "play dead." It's a feeling of being withdrawn, disconnected, and unmotivated. While the experience of clinical depression certainly exists in this state, it's common to experience being in shutdown without being depressed. When their kid is in the shutdown state, many parents make the mistake of assuming their child is lazy or doesn't care. It can be demoralizing to be stuck in this state, and frustrating for the person when others assume that they don't care enough. There are many possible shades to this state: feeling "meh," checked out, spacy, or tired.

THE ACTIVATED STATE

Moving up to the middle rungs of the ladder is the next, slightly more evolved sympathetic—or what I call "activated"—state. This state can happen when the amygdala hijacks the brain and sends a signal from the brainstem down to the sympathetic system in the middle of the spinal cord. This floods us with adrenaline and cortisol. We fight, flee, or freeze. We're mobilized, as blood rushes to our muscles. It's not easy to sleep or even just rest in an activated state. We're less patient and often talk too fast. We might be fidgety and active, or sleepless, staring at the ceiling at night. This is where anxiety and anger live. It's easy to see how the enhanced ability to fight or run increased our chances of survival. Other shades to this state may include feeling irritable, fidgety, nervous, hypervigilant, or overwhelmed. Most high-achieving perfectionists experience a chronic state of activation.

If your teen is in shutdown or activation and you try reasoning with them, threatening them, or even bribing them, your efforts will be in vain and may even escalate things, because your teen is in a state of survival and primed to fight and defend. It's not uncommon for a teen's nervous system to be out of sync with the reality of the moment. This is why the simple act of knocking on their door can send them tumbling down that nervous system ladder. It's up to us to help our kids (and ourselves) experience more regulation. That simple step can help them to learn new skills and good habits, build resilience, and most importantly, give and receive love and connection.

THE REGULATED STATE

Finally, the highest and most evolved state on the hierarchy is the experience of regulation. In this state, we might feel calm, peaceful, and connected—although we could just as easily feel more excitement and enthusiasm than calm. When we're regulated, we can easily give and receive affection. We can listen well, feel optimistic, and experience genuine joy and contentment. We might experience emotions like sadness or anger in this state, but these don't overwhelm us. You know this state when you're in it. It feels easy and not forced. You might also describe the experience in this state as peaceful, loving, open-hearted, joyful, or playful.

It's deeply satisfying to see our kids experience being regulated. They're genuinely happy, their bodies are relaxed, and they're engaged and receptive. For parents, seeing our teens in this state is the ultimate joy. Unfortunately, we will always get less of this than anyone else. This begs the question: Why does my teen seem so much more regulated with everyone but me?

This is so true. As parents, we get our kids at their worst. They seem to save the good stuff for everyone else.

This happens because our kids spend a great deal of energy shoring up, or trying to stay regulated in the world—or to at least act as if they are— because that's what is demanded of them. When they're home with the people they love and feel safest with, they're often exhausted from all of that effort. When they feel like they no longer have to put in this effort, they can quickly slide down the ladder, right before our eyes.

We do this too, don't we? Would your boss, neighbor, spouse, partner, best friend, or child describe you as behaving the same way at times? The only real difference is that, as adults, we're better at using our PFC to identify skills and practices to get ourselves back up the ladder. And of course when it comes to self-regulation, all of us are a work in progress.

Teens who are really struggling often perceive themselves as always depressed or anxious. They think they don't ever have moments of regulation. But we all have moments—or "glimmers," as Dana refers to them. Everyone. Encourage your child to look for those exceptions or brief moments, because they happen.

Parents often ask me: How do I know whether my teen is in the shutdown or the activated state, or whether it's just normal teen moodiness? Normal teen development involves lots of time in those shutdown and activated states. Teen moodiness, like adult moodiness, comes from one of the lower two states. But normal teen development also involves lots of time in a regulated state, particularly as they get older. Remember, the goal isn't an absence of those lower states; it's about flexibility and recovery. It's the kids who are stuck and can't seem to move out of lower states who should concern us. The ability to move back up toward regulation is a fundamental skill to learn. You can help your teen by first recognizing where *you* are on the ladder in any given moment. Ultimately, understanding why they are feeling a certain way is less important than building an understanding of what they're feeling. Becoming aware of what's happening moment by moment opens the door to effective solutions.

Principle 2: Neuroception

Most of us view others and the environment through the lens of our perception. My perception of something refers to my thoughts and mental representations of it; say, *That puppy is so cute, I hate all this rain, People in my neighborhood are really friendly, I'm enjoying this book.* But our perception of anything is actually not our first response.

The autonomic nervous system is like our personal security detail. It watches for cues of danger or safety, assesses them, and protects us as needed. The nervous system is the first responder to both our internal and external world, and it just wants us to be safe.

Perception follows close behind. Our perceptions are the story we create that follows the nervous system's initial response. I'll say more about this shortly.

Porges coined the term *neuroception* to describe the way our nervous system reacts to our environment. Here's a story to illustrate.

It was the spring of 2022, and my youngest child, then ten, was supposed to be on his usual ten-minute walk home from school. It was a couple of minutes past the time he would usually walk through the door. He didn't have a phone yet but had a simple smartwatch that he could use to call. Five minutes late and no call. My chest was getting tight. My heart was beating a little bit faster. At ten minutes, I was pacing and consumed with anxiety, as it was extremely rare for him to be late. My neuroception was perceiving danger. My perception followed, as I thought about the worst. Was he kidnapped? Was he somewhere being bullied, alone and scared?

I got in my car and drove to the park by his school. Nothing. My nervous system was braced to protect at all cost. I finally decided to call the mom of a close friend whom he often walked home from school with. This felt like my last gasp before I called the police, as it had been twenty minutes since school let out, and I didn't know where he was. The mom answered matter-of-factly: He'd gone with her daughter to their other friends' house after school. I called that mom, who let me know they were watching a show and eating a snack. My neuroception instantly shifted. My heart rate started to return to its baseline and my body to a state of regulation. I went to pick up my son, and on the way home we were able to have a positive coregulated conversation about safety and communication.

It was ultimately my neuroception, not my perception, that drove me during that long twenty-minute period.

STORY FOLLOWS STATE

Now that you know that the state of our nervous system is what drives us more than anything else, it's important to talk about the role of our thoughts, or what I often refer to as our stories. So here's another story.

One breezy spring evening a few years ago, I was cleaning up after dinner, listening to my Dancing in the Kitchen playlist, feeling regulated as could be, when I got a surprising call from a friend.

"Yshai, I'm really sorry to bother you, but I need your help; can you come over right now?"

She said her sixteen-year-old son, Tim, and his dad, Jay, were on the verge of an altercation, and she was afraid someone was going to get hurt. I arrived just in time. I knew walking into this that both Jay and Tim were going to be incredibly activated, which meant I had to stay regulated. The second I stepped in the door, I saw them in a standoff on the stairs. Operation "Get these two reregulated" commenced. First, I asked Jay to step away and let me hang out with Tim for a few minutes. I sat next to Tim on the stairs. I took some intentional breaths, trying to get my nervous system to speak to his. I used my voice as another tool to help Tim. In a calm, quiet, and kind tone, I said simply, "Hey, buddy." Tim was still breathing rapidly, still in a state of panic. I knew he would need to discharge some of his anxiety before we could talk, so I asked him if he'd go for a walk with me. I was relieved when he said "Sure."

As we walked toward a nearby park, Tim shared his activated stories. "I hate my dad. I swear to God, if he got any closer I was ready to kill him! He's such an asshole!"

Since Tim was so activated, I didn't know how seriously to take these stories. The combination of movement, my coregulation, and time helped Tim's nervous system settle. We sat on a park bench. I continued to manage my body and voice to offer coregulation. Instead of trying to solve his problem or offer a pep talk, I asked him how he was feeling in this moment. He said he was feeling better and his body was calmer.

From there we were able to have a thoughtful conversation that mostly involved me being curious and trying to understand. It turned out, Tim loved his dad and would never have wanted to hurt him. There were certainly some issues between the two of them that needed to get worked out, but it was nothing unmanageable. Tim talked about some of his worries and the depression he grappled with. He agreed to walk back to the house with me and have a conversation with his dad.

While we were gone, Jay had taken the time to calm his own nervous system. I helped them both listen to each other and begin the process of creating new stories. Jay was able to acknowledge that his intensity and impatience could be difficult to deal with at times. He affirmed that Tim wasn't a selfish or disrespectful kid. For his part, Tim was able to see how his language and behavior put his parents in a bind and could sometimes be frustrating.

As Tim and Jay's nervous systems regulated, their stories about themselves and one another changed as well, and they were able to experience coregulation. This is how stories and states work together. Our state affects our story, and our story responds to affect our state. It's a feedback loop that can be positive or negative.

At any moment, we all have stories about ourselves, others, and the world. These are our interpretations, opinions, and beliefs. A lot of popular self-help and even therapeutic advice focuses on changing thoughts as the first and primary step toward growth. This is sometimes referred to as a top-down approach to change. But it's not the most efficient path. If the communication between brain and body were a super-highway with five lanes, one of those lanes would be traveling north to south, from brain to body. The other four lanes travel south to north from body to brain. So yes, changing our thoughts absolutely helps, but the vast majority of change (80 percent) comes from the bottom up.

To put it succinctly, again, our story follows our state. Let's take a look at how this might show up in the three different states.

When I'm in a shutdown state, my thoughts about the state of the world tend to be more apathetic and hopeless. I have much less confidence in my personal sense of agency, and I tend to tune out. I will often avoid my responsibilities and can get fairly down on myself. In this state, I'm usually more socially isolated and withdrawn.

How does your child act when they're in shutdown? Are they avoiding schoolwork and other responsibilities? Are they spending excessive time on their phones or on gaming as a way to check out? They may give you only one- or two-word answers. For parents, it can be really frustrating and painfully difficult to try to help a child stuck in shutdown because it seems like they don't care about anything. It's important to remember that this is a terrible place for them as well. They know they're not doing well, but they don't know how to get out of it.

When I'm in an activated state, I interpret things differently. I tend to be more fearful or angry about the world around me. I'm more argumentative and less patient or tolerant of differences. I'm more likely to avoid new challenges out of fear. Just like in shutdown, I'm also not able to give or receive offers of connection from others. I talk faster, listen less, and sweat more.

How does your child behave when they're activated? Are they more angry and explosive? Rigid and inflexible? Argumentative or obsessive? It may be less obvious and easy to overlook when they're not misbehaving in this state. Many kids are getting good grades, hanging out with positive kids, and following all the rules—but many of them aren't regulated either. They're internalizing a lot of anxiety and are very activated. This is perfectionism. They're achieving at a high level primarily because they're terrified of failure and of letting others down (you especially). They rarely relax or enjoy their successes. Some of these kids can hang on for a while, but without intervention, it's only a matter of time before they slip or tumble down that ladder. This is why anxiety almost always precedes depression and the way back from depression moves back through anxiety

When I'm regulated, I'm able to see the best in people and have hope for the future. I'm patient, understanding, funny, and positive overall. I'm much more likely to not take things personally, and I more readily offer physical and verbal affection to the people I love. As a therapist, it's essential to show up in a regulated state for my clients.

RECOGNIZE YOUR OWN STATE

Like our fingerprints, we each have a unique nervous system. We typically don't choose our state in a given moment because it's an automatic process like breathing. We don't have to think about breathing or do it on purpose. However, we have a lot to gain by learning about how we breathe and paying more attention to it. We can benefit from using specific breath techniques to better our experiences. Understanding the nuances of our own nervous system and discovering ways to shift our state is a lifelong journey but an immensely rewarding one.

The next time you're on a walk or in a meeting, notice the way your body is scanning others and your environment for cues of safety or danger. Notice the tone of voice, facial expression, mannerisms, and dress of others you encounter. The colors of the walls, the art, and the décor. The smells, the sounds. All of it sends subconscious signals to your nervous system, which has its own unique way of responding to environmental input.

This applies to unconscious bias and racism as well. How our nervous system responds is based on context and prior experiences, whether directly from personal interactions or indirectly from media images. For example, several studies have found that, relative to their white peers, Black boys are more likely to be perceived as dangerous.[9] In a school setting, if the average teacher's nervous system is responding with more activation to Black students than to white students, it's no wonder that their stories are more negative and students of color are more likely to get referrals or suspensions relative to their white counterparts.

We all grew up being exposed and influenced by messaging about ourselves, people who are similar to us, and those who are different.

If I grow up seeing and hearing about people in ways that depict those with certain characteristics as scary, unpredictable, and deadly, then my nervous system is more likely to respond with activation when I see someone with those characteristics. In addition, I'll be much less interested in them or even capable of being curious about them and learning about all the good and important ways they contribute to our society. There will be a mismatch between what I know and what my nervous system is telling me. That nervous system, trying to protect me, will override my logic 80 percent of the time. We all do this to some extent when it comes to humans who are different from us in some way. It's just not easy to choose love or kindness or calm when we're activated.

Pause for a moment right now and check in with your nervous system.

- What do you notice? Do you feel calm and regulated? Anxious, energized, or fidgety? Bored, disconnected, meh?

- Notice where you are on that ladder right now. Wherever you are is okay. Perhaps what you've read so far has moved you out of a regulated state and you're feeling more anxious now because you're worried about not being good enough, or the struggles your teen is having. Or perhaps (and I hope) you are feeling more regulated and optimistic about both your teen and your abilities as a parent.

- As you read this, notice the space you're in right now. What cues are sending signals of safety and supporting regulation? As I write this, the hot cup of coffee beside me and the Jazz Vibes playlist in the background, combined with the soothing effect of the flowering houseplants nearby, are working together to help me focus and stay regulated.

- What circumstances make you more likely to slide down your ladder? It could be your teen's lying to you, or being disrespectful or aggressive. Or it could be unrelated to your child. Perhaps it's work stress that you bring home or a look or expression from the coparent you're feeling disconnected from.

- Do you tend to get stuck in shutdown or activation? We all have moments of feeling shutdown and activated, but most of us tend toward one state more than the other. The state we spend the most time in has a lot to do with genetics and our born temperament. The environment certainly influences it as well. As I've mentioned, flexibility within our nervous system states is key to our mental health. I sometimes get stuck in activation. When this happens for me, I'm usually overthinking, managing knots or butterflies in my stomach, and I'm more likely to get sweaty. I can be a bit of a nervous Nellie. This surprises many people, because I come off as calm and regulated on the outside most of the time.

- When you get stuck down there, what helps bring you back up to regulation? This is one of the most important questions for you and your teen to answer. Most of us have one or two go-tos that help us get regulated. It might be deep breaths, working out, video games (for teens), or Netflix. But most of us don't have enough coping skills. For many of us, our toolkit consists of a hammer, screwdriver, and tape measure. Those are great and essential tools to have, but they won't always meet the needs of the moment. Some of the tools in my kit include going to the gym, watching funny videos on YouTube, getting together with friends, spending time with my family, date night with my wife, getting out in nature, slow deep breaths, cleaning up a messy space, listening to music, watching a Blazers game, spending quality time with my kids, writing in my gratitude journal, and playing my ukelele. I encourage you to get started on your list as soon as possible and ask your teen to do the same. Once you get your list, hang it up in a visible place so that you can easily find it when you need it. Let's bulk up that toolkit!

• What do you notice about how your current state affects the way you think about yourself, others, and the world? Are you more critical and impatient on the middle and lower rungs? More loving, supportive, and optimistic when you're regulated?

The most important way to help your teen move up their own ladder is by staying regulated yourself in their presence.

As parents, it's essential that we work on building our capacity to meet our kids with a regulated nervous system. We can't fake this for long. Teens and preteens respond much less to what we say and much more to what our nervous system is communicating.

This is at the core of our job as parents: helping our kids learn to recover and return to regulation from an activated or shutdown state. All of the tips and strategies in this book are about helping you help them (and yourself) to do just that. For now, I'll offer a critical skill you can use to help your teen.

Principle 3: Coregulation

We begin life literally physically connected in the womb, separated only at birth. Then we rely on close emotional and physical contact to grow into healthy young humans. That sustaining instinct that we offered our babies to help them soothe is called *coregulation*. If you've adopted or fostered a child who didn't get that level of calm and loving attention when they were young, you've likely seen how much harder it is for them to self-regulate as they got older. This is something our foster son, James, has had to navigate, because *self-regulation*—the ability to calm and soothe ourself—is an outgrowth of coregulation. Newborns and toddlers who didn't get adequate coregulation from a parent or caregiver typically struggle with self-regulation when they get older.

But here's the thing: We never stop requiring a regulated other in our life to help us feel connected and okay inside.

In our American culture, we love self-regulation. We're taught to admire those who have pushed through their pain and made it on their own. We often think of these people as independent and tough. This is often what we want for our kids, too. Unfortunately, too many of us push our kids toward independence before they're ready. For example, we might take pride in their ability to make their own meal and get themselves ready for school in third grade, or their ability read a novel for hours by themself in fourth grade. When our little kids are dysregulated, we often put them in time-outs by themselves to self-regulate and "think about what they did." We love news stories about the young teen prodigies who enter college or profes-sional sports.

When we focus on what our kids are capable of and how they perform, we can lose sight of what they need. For good mental health, we all need an attuned and emotionally available other to coregulate with.

Of course, the goal of this transition to adulthood is increasing inde-pendence. All I'm saying is that we need to be mindful of our kid's emo-tional readiness and acknowledge that they will always need us, other adults, and their peers as coregulators in their life.

Take a moment to imagine a person in your present or past who has helped you regulate. It could be a partner, friend, or family member. It can be someone who's passed away who meant a lot to you. Notice how just thinking about that person brings a serenity and inner peace. Religion often serves this purpose. Experiencing symbols such as a cross or the Torah, a revered figure like the Buddha, or being in the presence of individuals like a pastor, priest, imam, or rabbi can help regulate our nervous system. Pets can be great coregulators too!

If your teen made a list of people who help them coregulate, would they put you on it?

If the answer is yes, that's fantastic. Just as often the answer is "It depends." But if their answer would be a solid no, it may be because you're going through a hard time. There may be very good reasons for you to be struggling right now. If you're managing an unhappy marriage; dealing with income, job, or housing insecurity; or working through your own childhood trauma, staying regulated with your teen isn't always possible.

So what you can strive for is improvement, not perfection. If you're able to get there 20 percent of the time, strive for 30 percent and improve gradually from there. None of us who are actively involved in our kids' lives are anywhere near 100 percent. Those who seem to be are likely either seeing their kids infrequently and therefore able to do just the fun stuff, or are fairly checked out and disengaged (lower rungs on the ladder).

Learning to self-regulate requires a steady stream of coregulation with others. Not just parents, but peers and other adults as well (I'll address these two groups in chapters 6 and 7). None of us can do this alone. As you know all too well, parenting is a grind, and as important as connection is, our teens can't learn to self-regulate without expectations and accountability as well.

As you do the work offered in parts 2 and 3 of this book and lead by example as you increasingly offer coregulation, your teen will notice the difference, and their behavior will improve. And don't be surprised if you see them getting better at self-regulation.

PART II

Connection
Is Up to You

Our well-being depends on many factors, including genetics, temperament, culture, environment, lifestyle, parenting, and trauma history. But by far the most important factor influencing our mental health is our degree of connectedness with others. As I mentioned in the introduction, on the whole, our teens are feeling disconnected and lonely. We have a responsibility to continue to figure out how to help.

This book is based on the premise that the source of the problems is not social media, bad/overparenting, or an entitled generation, but a lack of meaningful connection. Authentic connection with parents, peers, and other adults inoculates teens from the toxic elements of our culture while strengthening their capacity to avoid and withstand these inevitable aspects of life.

Bruce Perry is a psychiatrist who studies childhood trauma. In his best-selling book *What Happened to You*, coauthored with Oprah Winfrey, he speaks about the impact of loneliness: "One of our major findings is that in determining someone's current mental health, the history of their childhood relational health—their connectedness—is as important as, if not more important than, their history of adversity."[10] So as painful and awful as trauma is, the hurt is magnified in the face of isolation and loneliness.

This is big news. So many of us shield our kids from adversity, trying to protect them from heartbreak, rejection, failure, and pain. We need to realize that when we bolster our child's experience of belonging and connection, the difficult but inevitable aspects of life become much less harmful and debilitating over time. When met within a context of warmth and support, these painful experiences typically lead to greater resilience, character, and maturity.

As parents, this starts with us. I know, much easier said than done. Connecting with our teens can be elusive and feel difficult if not impossible. But that doesn't mean they need it any less. As the adults, it's our job to figure it out, and I'm going to help you do that.

Our teens desperately need connection in their life, connection that feels meaningful. There's nothing more important. Their mental health as adults is riding on it.

Meaningful relationships in adulthood are linked to countless positive outcomes, including longevity, lower risks of disease, and more happiness and well-being overall.[11] The need to grow and evolve and receive our love or support obviously doesn't end at age twenty-five. But the period from childhood to that age is the window in which our support and involvement will have the most impact.

We give our teens their best chance to be healthy and happy when we can develop and facilitate three types of connection: with us, with their peers, and with other adults.

In this part, in chapters 4 and 5 I'll show you how to create more connection with your teen as a parent or caregiver. Chapter 4 focuses on offering you some nuts-and-bolts strategies. Chapter 5 goes beyond strategies, providing you with an effective mindset to develop a deeper and more authentic connection with your teen. Chapter 6 shows you how to support and encourage healthy friendships, dating, and sibling relationships. Finally, chapter 7 explores how to support your teen's important and essential relationships with other adults.

CHAPTER 4

You:
Their Positive Relationship
with You Comes First

With the exception of a groggy stroll to the kitchen for breakfast at 1 p.m., Monica hasn't left her room all day. It's 4:30. Her mom, Michelle, knocks on her door.

"Can I come in?"

"Sure," Monica responds.

Michelle points out the obvious: "You haven't been out of your room all day."

Monica looks at her like her mother's already overstayed her welcome.

Michelle pushes past her anxiety: "You've been on your phone all day. I'd like you to turn it off and hang out downstairs with me."

Michelle's fears of both rejection and a fight are right below the surface, but she's trying to stay strong and calm. The five seconds before Monica responds feels like five minutes. Finally Monica responds, as though her mom is on a Facetime call and not in her room, six feet away.

"Fine, I'll come down in a little bit."

Michelle leaves feeling good about taking on that challenge and getting Monica out of her room.

One hour later...

Michelle's getting more frustrated by the minute. Just as she's ready to stomp upstairs and get into it, Monica slowly stumbles down the stairs, walks past Michelle on her way to the kitchen, and heads straight to the fridge. She pulls out some cheese and grabs some crackers from the cupboard.

With suppressed resentment in her voice, Michelle announces, "I've got dinner going; it should be ready in about half an hour. I'm making tacos, the kind you like."

Avoiding eye contact, Monica coolly responds, "Nice, I'm so hungry."

Awkward silence...

Michelle's racking her brain, wanting desperately to connect. "How's your day going?" she asks awkwardly.

Predictably, she's met with a "fine."

This shallow and uncomfortable interaction goes on until Monica finishes scarfing down dinner and returns to her room as though she's just completed her community service and is a free woman again, allowed to make her own choices.

Many parents like Michelle feel stuck in a catch-22 with their teenager. If Michelle brings up things like chores or school, they often end up arguing. Instead, she was trying to connect with Monica and not bring up those things, but that didn't go anywhere either. Sometimes Michelle feels discouraged and frustrated. This is when her predictable stories emerge. Is she a bad parent? Where did she go wrong? Other times she blames Monica for being spoiled, lazy, or just rude.

Can you relate?

I'll come back to Michelle and Monica at the end of this chapter and share how they were able to repair their connection. But first, let's talk about the nuts and bolts of connecting with teenagers.

One of the hardest parts of parenting teens is the amount of uncertainty we're forced to live with. None of us knows how our kids are going to turn out. Much of the time, we don't know if they're actually fine or whether there's something deeper and bigger needing to be addressed.

So we tend to worry. A lot. Some of us worry that our kids are going down a painful path similar to the one we went down at their age. Or perhaps we can't relate at all because we were so different back then. We worry that we've failed in some way. We worry that their future will be filled with pain and regret. We love them so much and are trying to protect and help them. We're just trying to be good parents.

But they may receive your good intentions in a different way. The more you worry, the more you will find yourself oscillating between activation and shutdown. As a result, your teen is less likely to see your love and more likely to perceive you as controlling, detached, fragile, or unreliable. They'll often manage these feelings by attempting to avoid you or avoid conflict by pleasing you, telling you what you want to hear. Alternatively, they may be throwing wrench after wrench at you, attempting to sabotage your every attempt at connection.

None of us wants that, of course. The antidote is more healthy and authentic connectedness. If that sounds a bit woo-woo, stay with me.

Connecting with our own teens sounds lovely. But as you know too well, in the real world it's often elusive and messy.

Most of us make it harder than it needs to be. I know you want more time with your teen or to be closer. The good news is, despite behavior to the contrary, they want the same thing!

But before we look at some specific strategies to strengthen our connection, it's important to acknowledge how we get in our own way.

Here are five ways that you may be inadvertently contributing to the disconnect. I know these well because I've done them all.

- When they pushed you away, you took it personally and withdrew in kind. When our feelings are hurt, we often have a way of shutting our kids out as a passive-aggressive punishment.

- You're too busy and distracted. So many of us are running ourselves ragged, stretched super thin and/or working too much. When this happens, it's inevitable that we'll miss opportunities to connect meaningfully with our kids. They can seem to be doing fine or even well. But in many cases, what looks like maturity and independence in kids is a cover for buried loneliness and anxiety.

- You've developed a narrative about your child that they're spoiled, manipulative, a jerk, selfish, or lazy. Even if you're not saying these things out loud, your teen's picking up on your demeanor and likely overhearing you talk to others about them.

- Your impatience is based on unrealistic expectations. Examples might be wanting them to show gratitude for all you do for them, being frustrated because they're not enjoying the hike, expecting them to be kind all the time or good at a chore that they just started doing.

- When your teen gets angry, you get into a power struggle or battle of wills with them, trying to assert authority by being louder or stronger or taking things away.

Every parent I know can identify with at least a couple of these.

There's one more reason you may be struggling to connect with your teen: Their mental health issues are so severe that they struggle to connect with anyone right now. They may have friends, but their bond relies on shared depression, anxiety, or trauma. If your teen is exhibiting any of the following, it's essential that you get professional help for them and your family:

- Missing significant amounts of school

- Lying a lot

- Self-harming

- Not spending time with offline friends

- Hanging out with delinquent friends (kids who skip school, frequently use drugs, break laws)

- Physical aggression

- Excessive isolation

Under these circumstances, it's essential to work with a family therapist who understands teens and supports parents without blaming them. In these cases, there is often not just the absence of connection; your teen may actively, although unintentionally, sabotage your connection with them. This is by far the most difficult situation to be in because your teen is internalizing so much pain that they can't help but project it onto you, which often results in your experiencing similar hurt and frustration. When they experience your negative response, it reinforces what they already believe to be true about themself. This self-perpetuating cycle can be very hard to break out of for both child and parent.

For these challenges and more, it's too easy to fall into resignation. Into a false belief that they don't need or want us in their lives. That we're no longer relevant or important to them. They may even say as much. But I hope you're starting to see that this behavior isn't so much a choice as a survival response dictated by their nervous system.

The essence of this book is helping you shape your teen's brain and nervous system in a way that gives them more experiences of regulation, which results in more access to their PFC. This will make it easier for them to become regulated, which makes it easier to access their PFC, which makes it easier to use self-regulation and coregulation strategies, which makes it easier for them to become regulated...you get it.

Regardless of your unique circumstances, know that there is no more important variable influencing their long-term happiness and mental health than the relationship they have with you.[12]

Now let's look at some specific strategies that will contribute to a more positive and authentic relationship with your teen. Remember, your teen wants to connect and spend time with you. But as you learned in part 1, the combination of their drive toward autonomy, developing brain, and frequent state of dysregulation can make this a bit tricky. We're not trying to control or manipulate their behavior. Our role is to be the adults and create a space and context that makes it more likely for them to be open and connected with us more of the time. The following five tips will help you get there.

Manage Your Nonverbal Communication

How did you feel the last time you were with your teen? Did you experience joy and pride? Anxiety? Irritation? Fear? Shutdown? Whatever the case, it's likely that your teen's nervous system picked up on the nonverbal messages that you were conveying far more than your outward behavior.

You may be familiar with the often-cited 93/7 rule of communication.[13] According to this rule, only 7 percent of our communication involves words; the rest is nonverbal. Of that 93 percent, approximately 55 percent is body language and 38 percent is voice and tone. When you factor in their developing PFC and sensitive amygdala—making it difficult to take in our words—I think that 93 percent is likely even higher for adolescents.

The moment you walk in the room, your teen's nervous system is responding to your face, eyes, posture, and voice. They instantly develop a story about these nonverbal cues. Your relationship with your teen right now is based in part on thousands of these micro interactions. Right or wrong, they've created a story about themself and you.

For example, if you come home from work at the end of a stressful day, you may be physically tense, short with your words, and preoccupied with more stuff you have to do later that night. There's nothing inherently wrong with that. You may be doing the best you can. What's your child's story about that? They may make it a point to steer clear of you, not wanting to cause you any more worry or stress. Or perhaps they're afraid that you'll snap at them. Some kids who are pleasers may go out of their way to try and make you feel better, putting your feelings ahead of their own.

So what's a good option for you in this case? Take time before you walk through the door to put your work stress away temporarily. Allow your body language and facial expression to convey that you're happy to see your kids. When first making contact, don't immediately start in with unmet responsibilities. Take a couple of slow, deep breaths, say hello, and ask them about their day. Better yet, talk with them about something they're into. Teens are much more likely to engage if the first question you ask isn't about school.

What if your nonverbal communication is actually conveying warmth and calm and it's still met with angst and rejection? One of the relational consequences of our kids' navigating their sense of independence and autonomy is that often they'll be in and out of connection. Sometimes they'll pull away, turn us down, be ungrateful and unkind. Then, seemingly out of nowhere, they'll be warm and kind and craving connection.

We need to make the effort to stay open and available. We need to be that buoy in the ocean and stay anchored. It can be helpful to have a mantra. Next time you're feeling a bit rejected or frustrated by your teen's behavior, try telling yourself something like *It's not personal* or *That's their amygdala.*

It's really normal and common for teens to be unaware of their own nonverbal communication and the impact it may have on others. Other times, they may be well aware but are leveraging it to experience a sense of power and control in the moment.

But building up this skill is also an important part of their developing self-awareness and healthy interpersonal skills.

Offer More Listening Than Lessoning

Most teens are used to being talked to—and at—by well-meaning adults who just want to help. They've been given endless directions, expectations, advice, and wisdom throughout their lives. As a result, many of them don't expect to be asked a genuine question, and when it happens, they have no idea what to say.

Listening is arguably the most undervalued life skill. Kids are taught communication skills. They give presentations, have group projects, and often get opportunities via debate clubs and mock trials. We give kids these common experiences to practice communicating effectively with others. This is all good. Of course we want our kids to have good communication skills.

But what do kids learn about *listening* from a young age? Whether it's in the classroom, at home, in sports or anywhere else, when we tell them to listen, often what we really want from them is to be quiet so we can talk. In American culture right now, the practice of listening appears to be on the verge of extinction. If we want our kids to carve out a better path forward, become open-minded and thoughtful humans, then we need to teach them to be better listeners. The best way to do this is to be better listeners ourselves.

What Does It Take to Be a Good Listener?

Good listening happens only in a ventral vagal state of regulation. We often miss opportunities to hear our kids out because we're too stressed, anxious, and/or preoccupied. Regulated listening is the anchor that helps bring our kids back.

Good listening requires effort. We have to *want* to listen. This requires our focus, time, and energy.

Good listening requires vulnerability. To really listen, we must be open to being wrong—or to being changed by the other person. Of course, sometimes the stuff coming out of our teen's mouth is utter nonsense. But in many cases they have creative solutions or unique perspectives that we hadn't considered. If your identity is wrapped up in being an authority figure or having power over your child, this one is going to be tough. The fact is, our kids *respect us more* when we admit mistakes, acknowledge their wisdom, and utilize their good ideas.

Fortunately, I won't ask you to sit in silence and stare at your teen until they have something to say. (Talk about cringey.) Let's discuss what this looks like in practice.

Here's what your child probably (hopefully) knows already: That you love them. That you just want them to try their best. That you're worried about them and want them to be safe. That they're smart and capable. So rather than repeating these reassurances, a more effective approach is to ask specific open-ended, multiple-choice, or follow-up questions.

Here are some examples of specific open-ended questions:

- "What are you hoping to do this weekend?"

- If they'll be going to a party, "What are you most looking forward to about it?"

- If the party's happened and something didn't go well, "What do you think are the most likely reasons?"

- "How was rehearsal today?" If that doesn't go anywhere, try some follow-up questions, like "What parts are you feeling more stressed or worried about?" "What aspects are you more excited or confident about?" "How are your lines coming?"

Here are some examples of multiple-choice questions:

- "I notice you've been playing a lot more Minecraft lately; what are you liking about it right now? Is it playing with friends? Are you building something that you're really into? Do you like the social part? The creative part? Both?"

- "I know you don't like school right now; was today a horrible day? Bad day? Or meh day? If it was meh, what made it slightly less bad?"

Follow-up questions are great because they demonstrate that you remembered a detail they shared with you previously:

- "How did it go talking to your teacher today?"

- "You guys had a rough game last night; how did practice go today?"

- "How's Susan doing? Is she back at school?"

A big part of strengthening connection involves paying attention to their interests. Are they trying to land a new trick on their skateboard? How's their Magic deck looking? What's something they'd like to do more of but haven't done in a while? Who are their favorite YouTubers or streamers? Do some research into the things your kid is into. Being informed will allow you to ask better questions, which will build your credibility and rapport.

If you're asking questions consistently, eventually your child will respond with some openness and authenticity. Often this will involve their sharing something that causes them distress or leaves you feeling slightly concerned. Do *not* try to fix their problem or instantly make them feel better. These are tough moments for a parent. Most teens (and adults) report that when they share hard things, they just want to be listened to, and they don't need someone to fix it. When we swoop in too fast, going into problem-solving mode, our kids get the impression that we don't really care about their feelings.

A lot of the effort to connect with teens can feel superficial and unimportant to us as adults, but it's important to them. Your interest, if it's genuine, will pay dividends down the road. Before you know it, if you're lucky, they'll come into your room to spill their guts, right when you're about to fall asleep.

As a therapist, my job is to help teenagers self-reflect and problem solve. To do that, I have to find ways to get them talking and opening up. Often, they actually don't know what they feel or how they think about things. Sometimes they just don't know how to put their thoughts into words. Other times they're so used to not being listened to that they talk and talk and talk, because tolerating silence and reflection causes way too much anxiety.

By approaching your teen with a calm presence, a genuine desire to ask questions and listen, and humility, you'll be surprised at what you get back in return.

It's entirely possible that you're doing the right things, and what you're bumping into is more about timing or trying to engage at the wrong place or the wrong time.

Find the Right Place and Time

The moods of an adolescent, particularly a young one, are anything but predictable. This makes it really hard to find a good time to connect. So it's important to know your child and look for the places and timing that work best for them, as well as know when to give them space and wait for another time. This can certainly be tough to gauge.

In general, don't call out your kid or try to connect with them in front of their friends. In these moments your teen may prefer that you simply not exist. Some kids don't want to talk about school right when they get home from school. Or right after they've downloaded to the other parent.

A lot of parents and teens tell me their relationship improved when they were able to find a shared activity and routine together. This could be a daily walk, making a meal together, volunteering together, watching a show, or spending time in the car. A lot of families I've worked with made a habit of following therapy with lunch or dinner out afterward. Predictability and consistency are your friends as you think about activities to do together.

As I described in the intro, my first job working with youth was at the Christie School, a residential treatment facility for traumatized kids. Most of the kids there had experienced profound neglect from caregivers, so they typically struggled to trust and connect with others. One effective way that we worked to counter this was by ensuring that every night before bed each kid got ten to fifteen minutes of undivided attention to do an activity with a specific staff person they had built a relationship with. This would typically include games like Mancala, cards, or just talking.

This single-focused attention with someone they trusted, or were learning to trust, was something they could count on, and it was never withheld due to poor behavior.

If you're in a rut with your teen and they seem to be taking a hard pass on any and all overtures, don't give up. In these situations, it's important to look for, and create, micro moments (there are always micro moments). These are the brief moments where your teen is open for business with you.

Keep It Short and Sweet

Many of us overtalk. We do this because we're uncomfortable with silence or we don't think our kids are listening or taking it in, so we keep going and repeat ourselves. Sometimes we keep talking because we're not picking up on their glazed-over look of *I get it, I feel trapped, and I can't wait for you to be done so I can leave.*

In addition to nonverbal communication, connecting with teens often involves frequent brief interactions. None of those short nightly check-ins at Christie School were game changers on their own. It was the cumulative effect over time that had an impact. It was an experience the kids could predict and rely on. It wasn't removed as a consequence if they misbehaved. No matter how stressful or chaotic their day was, they could always anticipate ten to fifteen minutes of coregulation with an adult who cared.

When we overtalk, teens tune us out, and we often lose credibility and influence. There are a variety of reasons for this. Sometimes they're overloaded with information and can't process everything we're saying. This ends up causing them a lot of stress and anxiety. Another reason is that they've heard this monologue before. They know what you're going to say before you say it. A third reason is that they feel talked down to, that their intelligence and knowledge isn't being respected.

Keeping it short and sweet when your child is shutdown or irritable might sound something like "You seem frustrated; let me know if there's anything I can do." That's it. Or you might simply say, "Good night, I know it was a hard day. I think tomorrow will be better. I love you." It might be coming into their room for a few minutes to say hi and ask them what they're up to, clarifying that you intend to stay for only a few minutes, and you're not there to make comments about their gross room, unfinished chores, or homework.

When offered sincerely, these brief moments accumulate. They demonstrate that we care and are paying attention. More importantly, we're communicating through our nervous system that we can handle their distress and conflict, that they don't overwhelm us. This helps them feel safer the next time.

To be clear, this effort is often very unrewarding. You shouldn't expect your teen to show any gratitude or appreciation for your efforts. None of these micro moments are game changers in and of themselves, but over time, the needle moves, and they'll start to talk and engage with you more. If reaching our kids is a baseball game, we're just trying to get on base, not to hit a home run.

The overarching goal of connecting with our teens is ensuring that they *feel* loved. It's not their job to make *us* feel like good parents.

As you offer more frequent, brief moments of connection with your teen, try to be mindful of your ratio of positive to negative comments. Teens need honest feedback and guidance, but positive reinforcement will always go further than negative comments.

Studies show that a ratio of at least three positive comments for every one negative or guidance-related comment is the best way to increase motivation, happiness, and compliance.[14] This applies not only to our kids but also to how we treat employees, friends, and even ourselves.

Offer Physical Affection and Touch

In one famous study by Jim Coan, a neuroscientist at the University of Virginia, women were given an fMRI scan.[15] They were informed that there was a 20-percent chance of receiving an electric shock on their ankle. While alone in the machine they reported high levels of emotional arousal. They were in fight-or-flight. In a second part, they were invited to hold the hand of a stranger. Doing this reduced their experience of pain. In a third part, they held the hand of their partner. While the shock was the same during all three trials, participants reported the least amount of emotional and physical pain when holding the hand of a loved one.

A study of NBA teams found that the most successful teams had higher rates of touch among the players.[16]

The physical and psychological benefits of physical touch are irrefutable. This is true from birth through old age. Physical touch from a trusted other reduces cortisol levels and physical pain. It moves people up their ladder.

So how do you connect with a teen who doesn't want to be touched?

It's important to appreciate the fact that some kids, particularly very sensitive ones, are less comfortable with physical touch in general, and that's okay. We never want to force this or insist on any type of physical touch that our child (or anyone) is uncomfortable with. Even though it's your own child, it's important to figure out what type of touch works for them, including where and when. A conversation about this has the added benefit of teaching your child that their boundaries are important and you respect them.

Sometimes physical affection can look like a hand on the shoulder, fist bump, or high five. Other times they'll lean on you while watching a movie on the couch. At times you may just have to be okay with a limp hug. Many teens get these needs met intuitively through the comfort of a weighted blanket and or a cuddly pet, or by snuggling or wrestling with friends.

When it comes to teenagers, we often get so consumed with and worried about whether they're having sex that we neglect to value and respect the fact that so many teens desperately crave physical touch. Most of them don't know about studies like Coan's; they just know that they want and need physical contact. Many teens figure out how to get these needs met one way or another.

If you have a child who's experienced trauma, particularly involving physical or sexual abuse, they may have a very different relationship to touch. They still need it as much as anyone else, but they may need to work through the trauma and slowly learn to experience touch as a positive and not a dangerous thing.

Praise the Traits That You Want to See Expand

There's a well-known adage that what you focus on expands. Look for examples of your teen being brave, kind, helpful, loyal, resilient, or a good friend. This kind of acknowledgment, when done authentically, goes a long way.

Earlier, I talked about a cycle of negativity that we often fall into with teens who are depressed or anxious. We may play into this by starting to look for the negative behavior we expect, seeking proof that they're untrustworthy or lazy or not trying.

If you want to see your child's behavior improve and to have more connection with them, you'll need to look for the exceptions. The moments when they cleaned up or did something helpful without being asked. When they sat down and stayed regulated for a conversation, when they willingly turned in their phone after the first request. Then offer praise. Don't overdo it; just let them know that you see it and appreciate it.

Your teen does a lot of good and thoughtful things. I know, they do much less for you than they do for everyone else. But still, they have moments, and if you want more of those moments, it's important that you notice and acknowledge them.

Revisiting Michelle and Monica

Let's get back to Michelle. She and Monica definitely had a rough patch for a year or two. But by Monica's senior year, they were tight and had the type of meaningful and honest relationship that every parent would want with their child.

What helped? Some of it had to do with simple time and maturity. As you learned about in chapter 2, Monica's PFC had matured a bit more, making her less reactive and impulsive, and thus allowing her to be more reflective and thoughtful.

But the biggest change was in Michelle. She had learned that Monica's behavior and struggles weren't personal or a reflection of her as a parent. She realized that they had both been living such busy and hurried lives that they never really made time to connect without feeling rushed or stressed. So she carved out time in different ways for them to slow down and hang out. During these times, they agreed on rules like no phones or talking about school or responsibilities. She also realized that she had been taking all the things Monica *does* do for granted. She listened more and became more curious. As Michelle did this, over time, Monica shared that she had been struggling with anxiety and cutting for several years but hadn't told her mom because she didn't want to worry her. This explained a lot of her moodiness and isolation.

The great relationship that Monica and Michelle formed wasn't based on having a perfect child. Monica still struggled at times with anxiety and would occasionally bottle things up. But she knew that her mom loved her despite her ongoing struggles. She felt connected and open with her mom, and as a result, her grades, social life, and self-esteem improved.

Consider That You May Be the Primary Source of Disconnection

Finally, it's important to acknowledge if you, not your teen, are the primary source of disconnection. Perhaps you've given up and are avoiding your child because at least when they're in their room, they're not contributing to the stress in the house. Maybe you've busied yourself with work or a to-do list and stopped looking for opportunities to connect. Sometimes we tell ourselves that if our teen doesn't want to spend time with us there's no point in forcing it. Sometimes our feelings are hurt, we're too angry, or we just get too stressed and anxious around our child. If you're struggling with sub-stance use disorder or major mental health issues, you will not be able to authentically connect with your teen without addressing these issues directly. If any of these examples are true for you, focus less on trying to get your teen to behave differently, and please get yourself the support and care you need and deserve. I have seen many parent-child relationships improve once a parent, or parents, addresses long-unacknowledged challenges, indi-vidually or as a couple.

Summary

Connecting with teens requires you to first look at the ways that you've contributed to the dynamic. Then keep these tips in mind:

- Manage your nonverbal communication.

- Offer more listening than lessoning.

- Find the right place and time.

- Keep it short and sweet.

- Offer physical affection and touch.

- Praise the traits that you want to see expand.

The tips in this chapter are intended to have a cumulative effect over time. You may feel like these suggestions aren't working—that is, they aren't having an immediate, obvious effect. Improving the connection with your teen will take patience, persistence, and support from others. You've surely made mistakes that have contributed to the problems; that's okay, we all have. All that matters right now is the unconditional love and support you show today. Your reading this book and continuing to learn, matters. Taking care of yourself so you have more to give your teen, matters. Keep going.

Now let's dig a bit deeper and take a look at what it means to get at the heart of a meaningful and authentic connection with your teen. You'll find that a lot of this will apply to your partner, friends, coworkers, and family members as well.

CHAPTER 5

The Mindset: How to Connect Authentically

In the last chapter, I shared some important strategies that will help you connect with your teen. But if you rely solely on those strategies, you may find that they don't work. Your teen may be skeptical or feel like you're using techniques to manipulate them and get them to change to do more of what you want. I don't want you and your teen to have just a good couple of months; I want you both to experience transformational change that endures.

This chapter isn't about strategies or techniques. Instead, this chapter is about developing an attitude or mindset. It's a way of being that will enhance the depth of connection, not just with your teen but with anyone in your life.

I'm going to share a simple but specific and powerful framework that is the foundation of my ability to connect with my clients and my own kids. I've seen it turn countless parent-child relationships around. Called PACE, it was created by Daniel Hughes, a brilliant psychologist who specializes in working with families, teens, and kids. His *Attachment-Focused Family Therapy* is one of the books that has most influenced me as a therapist.[17]

PACE stands for:

- **P**layfulness

- **A**cceptance

- **C**uriosity

- **E**mpathy

You can think of PACE as the four legs supporting an essential table that authentic connection rests on. Let's look at each leg in turn.

Playfulness

In Hughes's later book (with Jonathan Baylin), *Brain-Based Parenting*, the authors observe that "Playfulness conveys a sense of lightness, optimism, and confidence that whatever problems are being explored will be managed and the relationship will not be harmed."[18]

The first leg of the PACE table, playfulness, comes in many forms and works best when it's shared. Obvious examples are things like comedy shows, memes, and jokes. ("Whenever I do therapy with dogs, I always ask them to describe their childhood. They usually just tell me it was ruff." *Bada bing, bada boom!*) But playfulness isn't just about funny moments. Something as simple as a gentle smile can have an impact. Games—video, board, card, and so on—sports, and dancing are all examples of ways that we convey playfulness.

Research shows that play helps strengthen synapses in the PFC. Seeing us engage in playful ways signals to our kids that we're okay and all is well right now.[19] It conveys a sense of confidence and optimism while lowering the temperature in the room. It's regulating. Think about a time when you shared a joyful moment with a partner or good friend or one of your kids: Is there any stickier glue to bring people together?

From the instant I meet a new client in the waiting room through the first moments when we sit down and before I ask them anything serious, I always maintain a friendly smile and do my best to ensure that my body language conveys warmth and safety. I ask them what they enjoy doing for fun. I may spend five to twenty minutes talking with them only about things they enjoy. I do this deliberately, no matter the circumstances, because I know that their nervous system is assessing me, as it should. I make sure that my demeanor, the questions I ask, and the way I ask them always convey a sense of lightness and joy. This is an attitude of playfulness.

In many ways, playfulness and humor epitomize the language of teens. I know, sometimes their humor is offensive or feels too edgy or inappropriate to us. Or in many cases, we just don't get their humor. That's all okay, and normal too, because they're learning and testing boundaries to figure things out for themselves.

Sadly, many teens don't see their parents being playful or happy. Sometimes they see their parent being more playful only after having a drink or two. We often take ourselves too seriously and send the message that being an adult is a morose, stressful, and joyless experience.

If you find yourself struggling to find joy with your child, it may be because you're exhausted from handling so much of the emotionally draining day-to-day parenting duties. Perhaps you have a stressful job. Or you're dealing with health issues. Or your child is particularly challenging. All the more reason for you to find ways to be playful and lighthearted with your child. Both your nervous systems will thank you.

In coparenting situations, sometimes the differences between you can get exaggerated. One becomes overly serious and responsible, reflecting a perception that "someone has to be the grown-up." Meanwhile, the other parent perceives the serious one as too controlling or critical, so they overcorrect by being overly permissive and focusing on fun.

The fun parent will always win over the kid in the short term while setting up the parent who sets all the limits for more conflict with their child. Long term, however, the fun parent loses respect, and the stricter parent tends to gain more trust and credibility.

If you're the fun parent reading this, keep in mind that you're not just more fun than the other parent; you may also be taking on fewer of the hard responsibilities. This doesn't make you a bad person, parent, or partner, but it does put some responsibility on you to validate, empathize, and appreciate the other parent and think about whether you can help create a bit more balance, and if so, how.

If you're coparenting and recognize this dynamic, it won't be useful to blame the strict one *or* the fun one. The goal is for each of you to move closer to the middle, while accepting that you each contribute different strengths and weaknesses, which can make you a great team.

If you're a single parent, you may not have to navigate the complexity of coparenting, but you may feel pressure at times to be all things for your teen. In this case, it'll be important to leverage your strengths, accept your weaknesses while working on them, and make an effort to build up or leverage your community and other adults to give you and your teen support. The next chapter is dedicated to that topic.

When Playfulness and Humor Don't Work

I have a natural sense of humor; I like to joke around, and people close to me often tell me that I'm pretty funny. I see this as one of my strengths. But at times this aspect of my personality has come out with an edge to it and landed on others in a hurtful way. I've been given feedback about this, and I try to be mindful whenever I make a joke, particularly as I parent my kids.

Here are a few specific pitfalls to look out for:

- *The timing is off.* When your teen is in the throes of sadness, anxiety, anger, or other painful emotions, we may use humor to manage our own discomfort. This erodes connection. Show care, concern, and empathy until you see that their emotions are more settled.

- *You're trying too hard.* Don't try too hard to get their approval or force connection. They'll see through this, and they may end up laughing at you, not with you. Teens value authenticity above all else. They don't need us to be cool; they just need us to be ourselves.

- *Watch the sarcasm.* Sarcasm is one of those gray areas. It can be fun and connecting. At other times it can seem like it's connecting when it's actually creating more distance. And sometimes it's just another form of passive-aggressive behavior that ultimately hurts others. For example, your child may play a song that they really like. Your response may be something like, "No wonder your generation is so depressed." How such a comment lands with your child will completely depend on your relationship and their mood in that moment. If you're not sure how it landed, don't be afraid to come back and ask them. When in doubt, always check in, and if warranted, apologize. It makes a huge difference.

    If sarcasm is a primary way you connect with your kid, try a two-week sarcasm break and see what other kinds of playful communication can develop.

Again, playfulness isn't about being exceptionally funny or entertaining. It's about sharing joy with one another or at least offering it, even if they may not be able to receive it. Think about someone you know who's good at this. They're not passive-aggressive or making themselves the center of attention; they're genuine and lighthearted. Notice how just being in their presence moves you up a couple of rungs on your nervous system ladder.

But playfulness alone becomes shallow over time. It leaves relationships feeling hollowed out and void of meaning. This leads us to the next critical aspect of connection: acceptance.

Acceptance

In *Radical Acceptance: Embracing Your Life with the Heart of a Buddha*, Tara Brach notes, "Pain is not wrong. Reacting to pain as wrong initiates the trance of unworthiness. The moment we believe something is wrong, our world shrinks and we lose ourselves in the effort to combat the pain."[20]

Acceptance, the second of our four legs, is one of the most challenging and confusing skills, but mastering it may be the most important and instrumental task in front of us. There are many misconceptions about the notion of acceptance, so let's first get on the same page, because I think I know what you may be thinking.

We accept our kids when we understand that thoughts and feelings kept in the shadows can gradually become unrestrained pain that will ultimately ravage them and others.

But this is important: All *thoughts and feelings* are acceptable. All *behavior* is not.

As parents, we get so caught up in the behavior. But behavior is often the outgrowth of the thoughts and emotions that have been suppressed. You might say, "My child cussing at me is not acceptable." I agree. But I ask you to consider that leading up to that moment of cussing at you, your child has been feeling sad, depressed, angry, powerless, or any number of other thoughts and emotions that all were very much acceptable but never got expressed or validated.

Most of us have told our kids that we want them to come to us if they need help, and to be honest with us. But our kids respond based on what they see and observe, not what we tell them.

The following are some common sentiments that teens often share with me. What would it be like to hear these words from your own child?

I hate school, and I don't know if I want to graduate.

You care more about work and my sibling than about me.

I have suicidal thoughts sometimes.

It's all your fault.

When you and Mom fight, sometimes I get so angry at myself that I cut.

I enjoy smoking weed every once in a while.

Some teens are open with their parents about this stuff, while others tend to internalize it. One big reason they don't share things like this with parents has little to do with normal adolescent autonomy or privacy. I often hear kids say that they don't share these types of things with parents because they think their parents can't handle it. They want to protect their parents; they think it'll stress them out too much, or they'll get so anxious that their parents will start monitoring them 24/7 and they'll get treated like they're eight years old. Sometimes they anticipate that their parents will be mad at them, overreact, or even just ignore or minimize their concerns. Feeling dismissed by someone we love and invisible to them is worse than being yelled at.

Acceptance and commitment therapy (ACT) uses a metaphor called the unwanted guest that I sometimes share with clients. You can see an animation on YouTube that illustrates this nicely.[21] It depicts a person having a barbecue party. All his friends are there and everyone's having a good time. That is, until the unwanted guest arrives. This guest smells bad and is incredibly annoying. The host promptly kicks him out of the party. But he comes back until he gets kicked out again. But he keeps coming back. The host gets exhausted and fed up. Finally he tries a different tactic. He invites the unwanted guest and lets him be. The guest is of course very annoying again, but everyone just pays little attention and lets him do his thing. Soon, after not being given a lot of attention, the unwanted guest leaves voluntarily and doesn't return.

Of course, this unwanted guest represents those feelings and thoughts that we struggle to accept. Like the party host, we often go to great lengths to fend off those unwanted parts. Many of us have been doing it for so long that we've forgotten that they're even there and how much exhausting energy we put into shoving them away. Your teen is likely doing that. They're putting a lot of energy into trying to kick out those unwanted feelings and thoughts that they deem unacceptable. You may be unwittingly encouraging that. Remember, all thoughts and emotions are acceptable; all behavior is not.

Daniel Hughes writes: "Certain behaviors may not be accepted, but the thoughts, feelings, wishes, fantasies, and intentions that led to these behaviors are always accepted."[22]

Why Do We Struggle So Much with Acceptance?

Many of us link acceptance with approval or apathy. Applied to the self, this looks like *if I accept my own flaws then I'm okay with them and I won't get better*. Accepting these dark thoughts means *I'm complicit and fine with whatever behavior follows*. But accepting these parts of ourselves and our kids actually makes us less likely to act on them, not more. This can seem paradoxical because it is.

Despite years of my own therapy and lots of work on myself, I still experience anxiety in my life. The more anxious I am, the less accepting I am of my own kids' thoughts and emotions. My words and body language communicate *You'll be fine* or *That's not a big deal.* When I'm in my activated state, I'm more likely to counter their flawed arguments and show them why they're wrong. I can often see it while it's happening, but it's hard to stop. I'm not anchored, and the longer I engage, the more disconnected they get.

It's easy for me to be hard on myself about things like this and beat myself up. As a so-called "parent expert," I sometimes feel there are parts of me that feel hypocritical, and I sometimes struggle with imposter syndrome. Being able to accept these thoughts with compassion and honesty as they pop up is the only way I could have written a parenting book in the first place. It's important to be able to help our kids put words to these less appealing parts of themselves and for us to meet them with acceptance. Let's talk about how that might look.

Acceptance in Action

He Who Must Not Be Named elicited fear and terror by being mysterious and unknown, until Harry Potter had the courage to make everyone uncomfortable by asking, "You mean Voldemort?" As the saying goes, you've got to name it to tame it.

So what does this look like in real time? Here are a couple of examples.

In this example, the barrier to acceptance is the parent's need to problem solve and find a solution.

Teen: Mom, I think I'm depressed.

Mom: Maybe that's because you're spending too much time on your phone and staying up late. If you start going to bed earlier, I think you'll feel a lot better. Let's start going for more walks together.

Teen: [*not feeling heard or accepted*] Okay. [*Of course, then she doesn't follow through.*]

Mom: [*one week later, thinking to herself*] This is so frustrating. If she was really feeling depressed, she'd go to bed earlier and get more exercise. She's not even trying.

Teen: [*thinking to herself*] There's no point talking to my mom, because it's not helpful, and I feel worse. She doesn't get it.

Alternative with acceptance:

Teen: Mom, I think I'm depressed.

Mom: Sweetie, that sounds really hard and stressful. Thanks for telling me. Can I give you a hug?

[*They hug.*]

Mom: Would you like to talk about it a little bit, or would you rather not right now?

Instead of trying to find ways to help her daughter not feel depressed, she meets her where she's at, with acceptance.

Notice here: no fixing or problem solving; that will come naturally over time. For those of us who are really good fixers, this can be very very hard. But less talking and more listening is always helpful in supporting a teen to feel your acceptance.

Here's an example where the barrier to acceptance is the parent's ignoring the teen's concern and steamrolling right past them.

Teen: I hate school! It's pointless.

Parent: We all have to do things we don't like, and it's important for you to get into a good college.

Teen: [*walks away but internalizes*] I obviously know that; I just had a hard day, and you don't care or get it. I'll just talk to my friends from now on and tell you that school is going fine.

Interacting from a place of acceptance:

Teen: I hate school! It's pointless.

Parent: I'm really sorry you have to do something every day that feels pointless. It's okay to feel that way; I can totally relate. I felt that way at times about school, and I sometimes even feel that way about work. [*Notice whether imagining saying this makes you uneasy. Try to just accept that feeling.*]

Acceptance doesn't mean you always agree, but if you want your teen to be more open with you, you'll have to acknowledge their views and feelings and meet them where they're at. This level of acceptance naturally leads to the next step: curiosity.

Curiosity

So now that we've accepted their point of view or feelings without labeling or judging them as good or bad, right or wrong, we have an opportunity to establish the third leg of the table, which is to get curious.

Curiosity is one of those concepts that are so simple but so hard to practice in real time, especially with those closest to us. But it's imperative, if we want to experience authentic connection with our kids.

To do this well, we have to come from a place of no agenda other than to understand. We have to engage our inner scientist.

It's easy to throw curiosity out the window, replacing it with our knee-jerk assumptions in the moment. Sometimes we're correct, but when we're not, the price is high. In these situations, we can end up rupturing the very relationship we so desperately want to build.

Sometimes we don't even bother asking, because we *know*—or at least we think we do. She's out past curfew, and you're fuming. You *know* she's probably smoking weed or with a crowd you don't approve of. You *know* she's being selfish and disrespectful. You *know* all that time she's spending on her phone is because of an addiction.

This has been a hard one for me to learn. I've been a therapist for over twenty years and in the personal growth field for much longer. Why would I need to ask questions? Sure, I can pretend I don't know what's going on, but trust me, I get it. In fact, I know my kids better than they know themselves! I've got the answers, if they would just listen to me!

Parenting is a humbling experience. I was a way better parent before I had kids. My kids teach me every day that my vast array of knowledge and expertise means little if I don't stay curious and present. Apparently they're not interested in my advice, tips, or fantastic solutions. They just want to be heard and feel understood. Dang, that can be so unsatisfying! Long-term success at parenting requires humility. This means approaching problems with a beginner's mind. With not knowing. When I'm able to do this, it's amazing how much I learn about them and how my influence grows in turn.

Think about a time with your own child when you really listened with curiosity, and through that process you realized that there's more going on underneath their behavior than you had previously assumed. It's actually a really cool experience for a parent.

One area where I struggle the most is with teens who make self-destructive choices and also act overly confident and self-assured about it. A sixteen-year-old I met for the first time shared that he was smoking weed daily. He described this in an unapologetic, almost proud way. My knee-jerk reaction in those situations (I've been in too many of them) was to offer a "helpful" lecture about the impact that THC (the active component of marijuana) has on the developing PFC and how it affects learning and memory, and so on. While these facts are true and important, I had no connection, so all he was hearing was another adult lecturing, lessoning, and not getting him again.

I also used to make a lot of assumptions. I'd assume they're self-medicating to deal with their mental health or peer pressure. Assumptions lead to lectures, followed by superficial listening, more assumptions, and more lectures. Fortunately for my clients, I don't do that any more. I have discovered a much more effective approach.

What I typically do now is start with acceptance, acknowledging that this is where they're at; they think smoking weed every day is fine. Then, instead of my usual assumptions, I get curious. With genuine curiosity, I ask what motivates them to smoke. I asked questions like, "What do you like about it? Does smoking with that frequency feel like a good amount to you or too much? Are there different reasons for why you smoke (or vape)?" I ask such questions with a blank slate, truly not knowing and being interested in the answers. In this case it really paid off, because his answer surprised me.

He said he kind of likes smoking, and he does it for different reasons at different times. He then eagerly shared, "I smoke at night before bed because I get migraines and that's the only thing that seems to help. It also helps me sleep. I also get really anxious at night." This was super helpful for him to be able to say—and for me to hear. I could tell this was the first time he was able to share his experience without an adult jumping all over him with lectures about addiction or threats of consequences. The more I listened and stayed curious, the more he opened up. More than that, I could see him soften and become less defensive. This was a major step toward his eventual shift into wanting to smoke less and find other means of dealing with his migraines and sleep problems.

We make a lot of assumptions as parents. Don't get me wrong; we're often right. But sometimes we're wrong. Remember, being right doesn't matter. If our priority is connection, focusing on right and wrong is always a barrier.

Curiosity is about asking questions with a level of uncertainty about the answer. Genuine curiosity takes courage. It takes courage because it requires us to temporarily relinquish our power and authority and to tolerate the potential of being wrong and not knowing. Not knowing and uncertainty foster anxiety in many of us.

Genuine curiosity is really hard, particularly when it comes to the people we love the most. When we're anxious, angry, or shutdown, it's impossible.

Early Childhood Trauma Can Make Curiosity Very Difficult

If a teen has grown up with family conflict and/or trauma, expect them to struggle with their own curiosity. When you ask questions with genuine interest and an intent to understand, you may get little in return for a while. They aren't being oppositional or stubborn; they just don't know how to think in this way. Chronic stress and conflict in early childhood leads to a nervous system that is frequently in shutdown or activated. This severely limits their capacity for self-reflection and self-soothing.

If you're in a situation like this, it's really important that you stay the course. To repeat the lesson I shared in the intro, outlove 'em and outlast 'em. To endure and keep showing up, you'll need support for yourself. Your child will need help from therapists and other adults with the skills to listen and be curious. Often with kids like this, most people start out with playfulness, acceptance, and curiosity, but as soon as that falls short, they throw it all away and move on to a "tough love" approach. This typically involves a heavy dose of "tough" and very little "love." This is the opposite of what the child needs.

What Curiosity Can Look Like

Often, teens aren't being obstinate or stubborn, they just really don't know what to say. Sometimes it's helpful to offer a drop-down menu of possibilities. It's a way to get them to think about their experience without telling them how they feel. For example:

Dad: Natasha, you've been really short and distant lately. What's going on?

Natasha: Nothing. I'm fine.

Dad: [*offering a curiosity drop-down menu*] I'm wondering if you're feeling overwhelmed with school? Is there stuff going on with friends? *or* Your mom and I have been arguing more lately; I can see how that may be stressful as well. Do any of those fit? Or is there something else?

By offering this curiosity drop-down menu, at the very least your child will feel seen, because you're likely to be on target with one of your guesses. Best-case scenario, you've just given them permission to share more with you, because you've communicated with your tone and posture that these topics aren't taboo or off limits, and you can handle it.

Questions that come from a place of sincerity and humility convey respect and value to the other person. Even if your teen doesn't have a good answer or any answer at all, they will feel that you genuinely care. This will pay dividends down the road.

Here are a couple more examples:

Dad: I'm really just curious: Do you think our response was
           unreasonable?

Mom: You seem irritated. Are you still upset about what
           happened? It's okay if you are; I'm just wondering.

When we're able to hold this space of genuine interest and curiosity, it naturally deepens our sense of understanding their point of view in a new way. This paves the way toward empathy, the fourth leg of the table.

Empathy

Empathy is our capacity to feel some aspect of what another feels. It's a skill that takes practice and emotional effort, but there's nothing more transformative. Empathy and curiosity are interconnected. Without genuine curiosity, our attempt at empathy rings hollow. We may say the right words, but we're not resonating with the other person.

Do you ever wonder if your child lacks empathy? Of course, we've all been there. They get caught red-handed or did something that really caused harm to someone. In either case, they know what they did but just don't seem to care. Instead of remorse, you're being met with defensiveness or even disdain. A shrug of the shoulders or no emotion whatsoever. These moments can be very frustrating and concerning for a parent.

Once, when giving a talk to a group of parents, I was talking about PACE, and when I got to the empathy part, a mom raised her hand and asked, "How would I know if my daughter is incapable of empathy?" I ended up meeting with her family. I quickly discovered that they were clearly not receiving empathy, compassion, or consideration from their daughter at home. She was making some poor decisions and didn't seem to care, as she continued to repeat them. But when I met with her alone, it was a different story.

She shared that she felt depressed and that her parents labeled her as a bad kid (that doesn't mean it's true, but remember, perception is reality). When she talked about her friends or social justice issues, she lit up with all kinds of compassion and empathy. This teen had plenty of depth; she just couldn't access it around her parents. Her well-meaning and deeply loving parents had fallen into the trap of conflating her unacceptable behavior with being an unacceptable person. They'd stopped being curious and created a narrative that she was on the brink of becoming a sociopath, rather than a child in pain and in need of more support. They'd lost their capacity for empathy and curiosity. As a result, she felt more disconnected from her family and acted out more, which reinforced their notions about her character flaws, resulting in more anger on their end, leading them to up the ante with more threats and rejecting behavior.

I wish I had an inspiring outcome to share, but things didn't end well, and I ultimately wasn't able to help.

Some key points about empathy:

- *Empathy involves the ability to relate to the emotions of others.* Teens who seem to lack empathy and emotion on the surface typically have a large inner capacity for both (just watch how they are with a friend or a pet). The problem often stems from being overloaded and shut down from *too much* emotion stored up over time. Teens who struggle with managing their emotions also often have difficulty with empathy. The same goes for us.

- *Empathy cannot happen when we're activated.* If you're consumed by anxiety, anger, or fear, you won't be able to offer empathy, because your body is in survival mode. Tuning in to another person's experience requires a regulated nervous system.

- *Empathy requires vulnerability.* Vulnerability isn't just about emotions. It's about the courage to be changed by another person's experience. To admit wrongdoing or an error of thinking takes courage.

- *Empathy takes practice.* It's a muscle that gets stronger with more use.

- *Empathy involves emotional boundaries.* Staying up all night worrying about your child is not empathy, it's anxiety. Having emotional boundaries means I can resonate with your experience while still holding on to my own thoughts, feelings, and actions. We are not the same.

- *Empathy is not endorsement.* As with acceptance, we can empathize with someone's experience and still not approve of their behavior.

Take a moment right now to pause and reflect. Are you experiencing a bit more empathy for your teen based on what you've read so far? If you are, it's likely a result of staying curious and open to learning.

If you're one of those cynical readers, I can relate to you too. You might be thinking *This is too touchy-feely. Like, that all sounds nice in a book, but in the real world, my kid can be threatening, and they're failing out of school. How does this PACE thing stop that?* I totally appreciate that perspective, and I have those moments as well. You simply want this behavior to stop! You *need* it to stop. Then we can get to all that other stuff.

When I'm in that mode, I have no PACE.

I'm way too serious and intense (no lighthearted playfulness).

I just want my kid to be different (no acceptance).

I know what the problem is and what needs to be done (no curiosity).

I think my kid is an entitled, spoiled, rude, manipulative, lazy…(no empathy).

I want your teen's behavior to stop too. But I also want your teen to experience their twenties, thirties, and beyond with genuine joy and fulfillment. I want them to miss you when you're away and look forward to seeing you and visiting you. I want your adult child to have healthy and loving relationships. I want them to have genuine compassion for themself and others. To do the right thing, not because they're afraid of getting in trouble or to seek approval but because it's the right thing to do. This is a longer process, but it comes with a better and more durable outcome.

Meaningful, lasting, and authentic connection with our kids rests on the table held up by the four legs of PACE. Our teens need regular doses of playfulness, acceptance, curiosity, and empathy. Depending on how your child is doing, this can be very difficult. You may feel like you've tried this and it doesn't work. I encourage you to stick with it. As a bonus, I think you'll find that this process will benefit other relationships in your life as well.

We're all a work in progress, and none of us is equally good at each of the four elements. What are your strengths, and what do you find more challenging? Perhaps you're naturally more playful, but you struggle with accepting some of their views and perspectives on things. Or perhaps you're a great listener—staying curious and empathetic comes naturally to you— but you take yourself or your child too seriously at times.

Your connection and relationship with your teen is the most important step toward building up their capacity for resilience and joy. It also sets the tone for the quality of relationships they will form with their peers. The subject of the next chapter.

CHAPTER 6

Peers: Their Second Family Is a Big Deal

Kate was in the middle of her eighth-grade year. For the past month, her parents had observed a noticeable shift in her behavior. She was more shutdown, withdrawn, and irritable. They were worried and didn't know how to help, so they called me.

When I met with them as a family, Kate was open and shared some context. Her two best friends were Maggie and Lisa. They had been close since kindergarten. The previous summer, Maggie and Lisa had started hanging out more and more without Kate. Kate didn't want to seem jealous or clingy, so she ignored the message her nervous system was sending, that their dynamics were shifting. At the beginning of the school year, the three of them hung out together like old times, but as the weeks and months wore on, Maggie and Lisa began drifting away again. Kate would overhear them talking about a hangout they had over the weekend that she wasn't invited to. They would talk to each other as though she wasn't there. Kate had some other friends, but these two were her people. She wasn't nearly as close to anyone else at her school.

Then she shared the incident that had sent her spiraling. Kate had a shared group chat with Maggie, Lisa, and several other friends. On a Sunday afternoon in January, Maggie shared a photo from her birthday party the day before. The kids there were goofy and clearly having a blast. Kate wasn't in the picture because she wasn't there. She hadn't been invited; she hadn't even known about the party. In about one second, Kate went from regulated to activated. She was instantly flooded with emotions. She felt embarrassed and humiliated. She was angry and deeply sad. She immediately dropped out of the group chat. The thought of going to school the next day filled her with anxiety and dread. She oscillated between hating herself and hating them. Kate couldn't regulate. She had a history of cutting under circumstances like these, and she was tempted, but she was working on using other coping skills, and her parents were getting better at listening without reacting, so she decided to try talking to them first.

Her parents encouraged her to talk to Maggie about it. Her well-intentioned mom lovingly told her that she's an amazing kid, she didn't deserve this, and it was her friends' loss. This didn't help Kate feel better, because she certainly didn't feel like an amazing kid.

Kate was too intimidated to talk to Maggie or Lisa in person. Instead, she texted the two of them asking them why she hadn't been invited to the party and telling them how she felt seeing that picture. The response from Maggie was short and shallow: "Sorry, I didn't think you'd want to come because Jane was there and I thought you didn't like her. I'm sorry I sent that picture."

Kate then summoned the courage to ask about the changing dynamic: "It seems like you guys both have been ignoring me lately. Did I do something?" Lisa chimed in, "No you're good, it seems like we just have been growing apart and have had different interests for a while."

The more Kate engaged, the more she found herself shutting down. She spent the rest of her Sunday mostly crying. Her parents felt heartbroken and angry that these friends she'd had for so long would treat her this way. They tried their best to console her but mostly felt helpless.

The rest of eighth grade was hard for Kate, but she did find some new friends. In high school she turned a corner and met a couple of *people she clicked with. Through that painful experience, she was able to fine-tune her values and the qualities she was looking for in a friend. She was no longer angry at Maggie or Lisa; she realized that they were growing apart for good reasons. Maggie and Lisa were increasingly drawn to a more popular crowd; they enjoyed parties and a bit more of an edgy scene. Kate learned to embrace the part of her that was more of a nerd and not interested in the whole party scene. Kate, Maggie, and Lisa were able to remain casual friends in high school, though they wouldn't be close again. Maggie and Lisa both ended up regretting the way they had treated Kate, and although they continued to grow apart, in ninth grade they made an effort to be kind to her. Kate appreciated their gestures and was ultimately glad to find a new group of friends that she genuinely valued and had fun with. Kate made it through a very normal, but incredibly hard part of childhood: important friendships shifting and growing apart.*

They're Separating, and It's Not Personal

For your teen, a positive and meaningful relationship with you is foundational. It provides them with a sense of identity and values and a safe place to fall. But during adolescence, the significance of peers can't be overstated. These relationships have the potential to make or break a teen's self-esteem and mental health. An attitude of PACE will help you understand and support the often complex dynamics with their friends and will go a long way toward helping them cultivate solid relationships.

Connection to parents and peers isn't a zero-sum game. Teens who are connected to their friends while remaining close to their parents have the best outcomes. In fact, studies show that teens who feel close to their parents are less likely to be influenced by peers who use drugs or alcohol and are more likely to be influenced by peers who excel academically.[23]

No matter what kind of relationship the two of you have, your teen should be spending less time with you. When they're with their friends, not only are you not the priority, but they may find the very way you breathe offensive. It's not personal. If you find this difficult, practice repeating to yourself over and over again *This is not about me.* When my daughter's friends are around, she generally doesn't want me to be around too. I may land a joke that a friend finds funny, but I'll still get an eye roll from her. To be honest, my feelings do get mildly hurt at times when my daughter doesn't seem to want to be seen in public with me. But then I remind myself of the simple truth that I will remind you of as well: Your child loves and needs you but is also developmentally wired to prioritize their friends right now. If it was the other way around, and they ignored their friends so that they could spend more time with you, that would be a problem.

Making Sense of Your Teen's Social World

How would you describe your child's peer world? Do they have a large group of friends? A couple of close ones? No friends? Are they all online? Do they spend time with kids who bring out the best in them, or are they with kids who aren't doing so well? Perhaps it's a mixed bag—or maybe you have no idea.

Peers have a different type of influence from parents. We have the most impact when it comes to foundational things like values and ethics. But when it comes to things like tastes and preferences, such as clothing, music, or hobbies, peers have much more sway. It's important to keep this in mind, because it's so easy to conflate the music they listen to or the clothes they choose with their values. But that's a mistake, because they're very separate. Some of the kindest and most thoughtful kids I've worked with wore all black, skateboarded, and had nose piercings. Similarly, I've met plenty of well-dressed, clean-cut A students who could be pretty unkind and dishonest.

Peers are important for other reasons as well. They help our kids try on different identities and personas. They expose one another to new experiences. They play, laugh, and create together. They support and care for each other. Despite the bad rap this generation gets—which is not just bad, but inaccurate—studies show that they're more likely to volunteer and to get involved in causes they care about, such as climate change and social justice issues.[24]

They're also very open about mental health. This topic is no longer taboo the way it was when we grew up. In one large national survey, 70 percent of teens reported mental health as a major concern among their peers.[25] How many of us would have benefited from being able to safely talk about our mental health challenges as teens? Friends provide a lot of essential coregulation for one another.

At the same time, peer relationships can be dysregulating as well. Adolescents who are mired in shutdown and activation have a way of finding each other. So many teens are hurting and being hurt.

One of the core challenges of being a teenager is striking the important balance between being true to themselves and needing to fit in. One of the core challenges of being a parent is figuring out how to help our teen experience more of the positive aspects of teen culture and less of the harmful and isolating aspects. So how can we best meet this challenge?

Their Friends Aren't Bad Kids

To begin with, it's important to reframe the way we think about kids with behaviors we object to. The vast majority of teens who make bad choices are really nice kids. They might be dealing with major mental health issues, difficult circumstances at home, or hidden disabilities. It's easy to write these kids off as "bad kids" and to judge them and their parents, but that's not helpful, for two main reasons.

First, when you criticize the kids your child hangs out with, you're inadvertently criticizing your child as well, because they don't think they're that much different from those kids (or they wouldn't be spending so much time with them). It's also extremely stressful for teens who feel like they have to choose between their friends or partner and their parents. Finally, the way you talk about their friends sends a signal about how you will think of them if or when they make bad choices or go through hard things.

The second problem with labeling other teens as bad is that it doesn't model empathy or compassion. Teens are often much better than we are at trying to see the good in others. They see the poor judgment and problems, but they also see the kindness, loyalty, and struggle that their peers are going through.

Avoid labels such as "bad kids" "bully," "victim," "offender," "stoner," and the like. It's natural for teens to group up with others who look, think, or act similarly. Too many of our kids put themselves in a box based on who they hang out with, and it's really limiting. It's important to help our kids think about and consider the nuance and complexity of people. Many bullies were once victims. Many people who are written off as bullies had one bad day when they acted out and then feel horrible about what they'd done. Many skaters don't like weed and get good grades; many jocks don't like the party scene and prefer to play *Dungeons and Dragons*. When we label our kids' friends, we also label our kids. Humanizing others is always a better way to go in our culture that would prefer to keep things in stereotyped categories.

Dopamine and Risk-Taking

Eric is typical of many sixteen-year-old teen boys I work with. He gets decent grades, is respectful, and has a pretty good relationship with his parents. Eric has a job on weekends as a golf caddy and shows up reliably. So why are kids like Eric referred to me? Eric's parents reached out to me because Eric was caught multiple times getting into trouble with his friends. Sometimes they'd climb onto the rooftops of abandoned buildings or spray graffiti on property, and occasionally they'd find themselves getting into a fight at a park. Despite my many years of working with teenagers, this behavior continues to intrigue me. It just does not match with the kind, thoughtful, and intelligent young person sitting across from me.

So I asked Eric about this discrepancy. Is he just BSing me? Is one of these two parts the "real" him?

Eric was as confused as I was. He didn't get it either. He acknowledged that he gets caught up in the moment and that it is kind of fun. He also admits that he regrets it afterward and knows that it's pretty stupid.

In these situations, I always make a point of giving teens and their parents psychoeducation about the impact of dopamine and peers. There were two different Erics. Both were real. He truly was a thoughtful and nice kid, and he did some stupid things while with his friends. These types of poor decisions never happened when he was by himself. If you're thinking that this sounds a lot like Brianna from chapter 2, you'd be correct. Risk-taking with peers is like peanut butter and jelly: They always seem to find their way to each other.

In many states in this country, teens can get their driver's license at age sixteen but are not allowed to drive with other teens in the car for six months. This practical law is grounded in some important science about how teens act with peers.

In one famous study, teenagers played a car simulator game in a lab while their brains were being scanned with fMRI.[26] They played the game alone and again while their friends were watching. When playing alone, they didn't release much dopamine and as a result took few risks running yellow lights. When they knew peers were watching, their behavior changed quite a bit. They released more dopamine and took more risks on the road.

Interestingly, the researchers also ran these experiments with parents observing and a mix of parents and peers. Teens took more risks only when they were being watched by their peers exclusively. This effect also doesn't happen for adults who are with their friends. Only the circumstances of teens with peers alone led to increased risk-taking.

Of course, this experiment isn't just about driving. These types of studies have been replicated and apply to all types of environments. When teens are together unsupervised, they're more likely to take risks.

Teens release more dopamine in the presence of peers. Dopamine and risk-taking often go hand in hand for adolescents. If your state has a law requiring sixteen-year-olds to wait six months before inviting friends to ride along in the car, be grateful; it definitely saves lives.

Don't Be Your Teen's Best Friend

Many of us were really tight with our kids when they were younger. As our children mature and drift away from us and toward friends, this can feel like a tremendous loss. But they need to develop more autonomy, and one way they do this is by prioritizing their friends. Our children need our guidance, wisdom, and emotional support in different ways as they grow, but not our friendship (that shift comes in their twenties).

After more than twenty-five years of working with teens, I'm just not as cool as I used to be (I never was actually cool). I wear sweaters, have gray hair, and regularly take Advil for back and leg soreness. I don't even have any tattoos. But I've discovered that teens still connect with me and value the relationships we form, because I'm a reliable and trustworthy adult who cares and listens. They don't need me to be cool, or to listen to the same music as them, or be a gamer; they want to be able to trust me and feel like I'm helpful.

Rethinking Peer Pressure

Many of us have a fear that our child is being, or will be, pressured into doing something they don't want to do. Perhaps they'll be manipulated by phrases like "Come on, everyone's doing it" or "Don't be a wuss." But it's not likely that your teen is an innocent baby lamb who has been pressured into antisocial behavior by a powerful and coercive gang of wolves.

Teens do care about what their peers think. They often do things that others are doing, not because they're being pressured, although this does happen, but usually because they want to fit in and be a part of a group. Far from being dysfunctional, belonging to your group is an evolutionary necessity. It's very healthy and adaptive. All teens are influenced by peers, but phase 1 adolescents are particularly susceptible to this influence.

Peer influence can be negative or positive. You now know that teens are more likely to take harmful risks when in the presence of their peers. The inverse is also true. They're more likely to make better decisions when their friends are acting in prosocial ways.

I encourage you to also consider that while your child's friend may be a bad influence, your child may also be a bad influence on their friend at times. Peers find each other based on mutual interests and relatability. Depressed teens typically hang out with other depressed teens. Academically focused teens typically hang out with academically focused teens. Don't automatically blame the other "bad influence." Changing schools or moving to a new town may not change this dynamic. Instead, focus on helping your teen get healthy, and if their current group is unhealthy for them, they'll move on to another group naturally over time.

So how can we increase the odds of their being exposed to positive peer influence? I have some specific strategies to offer. But I can't emphasize enough that the type of kids your child hangs out with is strongly correlated with the quality of relationship they have with you. If you don't have a good relationship with your teen, the risk of their having unhealthy relationships with peers increases a lot. If you feel like you have a strong connection with your teen and they're still drawn to negative peers, it may just be a phase of experimentation that they will eventually work through.

How to Support Meaningful Connection Between Your Teen and Their Peers

Your teen has a relationship with peers and always will. The important question is, what kind? Ideal relationships are ones in which kids can be themselves, feel safe, and experience joy. They strike a balance of being both online and offline. Relationships to avoid are those that breed anxiety, sadness, and more loneliness.

Teens who feel lonely and isolated are more likely to settle and find themselves drawn to anyone they perceive will accept them, even when the relationship proves to be harmful physically or emotionally.

To some extent, all teens and young adults will have to go through difficult relationship experiences on their journey toward more maturity and growth. That being said, there are a number of ways that we can help our kids develop more meaningful and healthy relationships with others.

Get to Know Their Friends

Sometimes it can be easier to connect with our teen's friends than with our own child directly. Our kids respond and appreciate it when we show their friends love and respect. It's an effective and indirect way to show them that same love and respect. This is harder, but even more impactful, when we don't care much for the person they're hanging out with. In these cases, your teen knows you're not a fan of their friend. When they see you making an effort to be positive and accepting anyway, it frees them up and accelerates their process of viewing this unhealthy friendship for what it is and moving on.

Develop Relationships with the Parents of Your Teen's Friends When Possible

Given the predictable amount of misunderstandings, hurt, confusion, and frustration our kids are going to experience with their peers, it's vital that we get to know the other parents when possible. To do this, we have to get past our own judgments and assumptions about the friend and the friend's parents. Assume that the parent whose kid is making bad choices loves their kid just as much as you love yours. If you're supportive and collaborative, you're likely to get the same in return. Working together with other parents makes it so much easier to enforce curfews and rules. Kids feel safer and more emotionally contained in communities where they know parents support and talk to one another.

Be aware. Sometimes your child's friend may disclose some concerning accusations about their own parents' behavior. You may find yourself feeling really bad for this kid. In these cases, it's important to be compassionate, but also to not let yourself get drawn in. The harsh things that kid says about their parents may be true, partially true, or not true at all. Regardless, you need to assume that the kid loves their parents and needs support to figure out how to develop a safe and loving relationship. Kids get to bash their own parents when they're mad, but we don't. Our job is to support repair and reconciliation to the extent possible.

Acknowledge Some Common Differences Between Girls and Boys

Teens are ahead of a new learning curve that's redefining the way we think about gender. It can certainly be difficult to keep up with the terms and pronouns that teens identify with. To be honest, as a parent and therapist at times I feel confused and awkward about navigating these new terms and gender expressions with this shifting ground. But it's our responsibility to learn and be open to the aspects of identity that are important to our kids. In many cases, the connection we have with them depends on our willingness to learn about these perspectives with an open mind.

Before I talk a little about some differences between boys and girls, it's important to note that the differences within genders is far greater that the average difference between genders. For example, on average boys spend more time on YouTube than girls. But the range of YouTube watching among boys is much broader than the comparatively small difference between boys and girls. Even using terms like boys and girls often requires more nuance, as some are cisgender, some are transgender. Increasingly, some teens feel like they don't fit into either category and increasingly identify as nonbinary, or somewhere in the middle, or more fluid and fluctuating.

I hope you find the essence of this section helpful and take what feels applicable to your teen. I'll be referring to boys and girls here, anticipating that the oversimplification provides more help then hindrance.

Respect Your Son's Desire to Be Loving and Caring with His Male Friends

Boys, in general, do relate to others differently from girls. They're more likely to connect through activities and to be physical with one another. It's often said that boys connect shoulder to shoulder more than face to face. But boys crave meaningful and authentic relationships just as much as girls do. As a culture, we still mock boys for being too sensitive or soft, or for wanting to have a deeper conversation with someone. Sometimes these messages are communicated directly, but they're nearly always expressed covertly. They show up in endless jokes and media images, locker room talk, and toxic coaches. Stoic men and emotional women are still the stereotypes in our culture. Boys wanting to connect with those softer sides of themselves typically hang out with girls. We need to remind our sons that expressing care and concern for another guy is super healthy and makes them *more* solid and resilient as a man, not less. This responsibility falls primarily on dads and men. As a dad, I have to constantly check my conditioning with my son. I try to remember to praise him when he expresses authentic emotions or cries and to resist the outdated notion that he needs to toughen up to avoid being perceived as weak among his male peers. If you're not lucky enough to have a man like this in your child's life, do your best to have conversations and expose him to movies and media images that show a diverse range of masculinity.

Address the Unreasonable Societal Expectations Put on Girls to Do It All

Girls are, on average, more social than boys, and they spend much more time on social media. This also means that they're more susceptible to relationship stress, competing, and comparing. The typical girl is expected to be kind, pretty, smart, funny, chill, ambitious, social, and strong, and to change the world, all at the same time. Friendship ruptures can be deeply painful and leave girls feeling like a failure. Whether it's online or offline, when your daughter experiences distress, take her feelings seriously. Yes, she will be okay over time, but while she's in it, it doesn't feel like it. Girls need social media breaks and limits to help them manage the seemingly endless stream of social engagement that is both fun and anxiety producing. (Boys are more likely to need breaks and limits with gaming.) You can help by validating the complexities your daughter is dealing with, including when it comes to social media. Then provide reassurance and talk with her about the value of her perceived imperfections and flaws. Help her define attractiveness by her own standards. If she talks back to you or challenges you, appreciate the assertiveness evidenced by the "unladylike" behavior. This will serve her in the future.

In general, observe the ways you respond to your son or daughter in different contexts—school, sexual relationships, curfews, and drug or alcohol issues. Ask yourself: *Would I be responding this way if it was my [child of the other gender] doing this same thing?*

Take the Drama Seriously

To us it may be drama; to them, it's real life. When your teen criticizes or bashes someone they normally care about, avoid jumping to conclusions.

Don't try to fix it or jump on the hate bandwagon. Instead, ask questions to understand more about where they're coming from, validate their emotions, and ask them how they want to handle it. It might be a relationship that needs to end, but they could also go back to being good friends or dating in a week. Be caring, but stay out of the way unless it truly feels dangerous.

It's also important to empathize with the emotional roller coaster that typifies young adolescent friendships. Adolescents are extra sensitive and aware of social status and where they fit in. They want to be true to themselves, but they desperately need to belong and have friends. Kids are often dismissive, rude, or unreliable because they're anxious or socially unskilled—not because they're mean. Anytime you put a group of adolescents together with a mix of intense emotions, a dash of mental health issues, minimal life experience, and social media that amplifies differences and comparisons, things are going to get messy.

Are Online Friendships Real?

Connecting online through gaming, social media, and the like is real and an important aspect of community for most teens and young adults (though it is not adequate on its own). Like it or not, it is a natural way for this generation to connect. Particularly for marginalized people or those with unique interests, online connections offer a validating and important way to feel less alone. So it's important to try to get to know about your teen's online social life the same way you would their offline one. It can be helpful to ask questions like these:

- "Who are some of your friends?"

- "How would you know if someone was fake or trying to take advantage of you?"

- "Do you have a best friend online?"

- "What do you feel like I don't get about your online friends?"

- "Do you think it would be good to have more friends you see in person?"

If all your teen's friends seem to be online, or they seem to be avoiding their in-person friends in favor of virtual connections, you're right to be concerned. But it will take time to help them find more balance by seeing or making friends in person.

As I've mentioned, the first step is to get to know their online friends. When they talk about their friend Jay who lives in another state, you may picture Jay as the fifty-year-old predator who's grooming them. But the friends they have online are probably not the people you're imagining. Having said that, be sure to talk with your teen about scams, when and whether to give money, and the importance of never giving out their address or personal info. There certainly are predators online. Older teens get this, but younger teens and preteens often don't think about these things.

Our foster son, James, now in his late twenties, used to give a lot of money away to "friends" online. He has since learned how and when to determine people's true intentions. But he had to make some mistakes, combined with a tremendous amount of coaching and emotional support on our part, to help him get there. Eventually he did, and he has become surprisingly good at setting boundaries in his online community.

Once you have a sense of the landscape of your teen's online social life, you'll have more credibility to talk with them about the importance of offline friends.

Lisa Damour, author of *The Emotional Lives of Teenagers*, likes to say, "Friends aren't made, they're found."[27] The key with these kids is to first try to uncover their fears or concerns about socializing in person. Often social anxiety and/or the habit and comfort of not leaving their room play a role in their hesitancy to engage with their peers. Then the goal should be to put them in positions where they find friends with similar interests. Sports are great for this, as are most clubs. Meeting new people or reconnecting with friends from the past takes energy and some tolerance for awkwardness, and it evokes a bit of stress. Your teen may be avoiding those experiences and feelings more than avoiding the people themselves.

So stick with it and persist with a nonnegotiable expectation that your teen get involved in some sort of extracurricular activity of their choosing that gets them out of the house. This will expose them to other teens with similar interests, which will significantly increase the odds of their finding a friend.

Dating in a New Age

First, we need to dispel the myth that teen boys want only sex. This doesn't bear out in the research, and it vastly undersells them.[28] As I stated earlier, boys want emotional connection just as much as girls do. Too often, they just don't know how to seek it out or even receive it. Boys' emotional intimacy skills lag behind girls'. This is largely a socialization issue, thanks to endless exposure to media images depicting men as superficial and shallow. But it's also developmental, as boys generally mature a bit slower than girls do. Also, boys typically don't practice emotional intimacy skills with their male friends the way girls often do growing up.

For adolescents, romantic relationships are an outgrowth of their relationships with parents and peers. They're also influenced by the megaphone that is the culture they grow up in. Avoiding this topic as a parent and relying on the fact, or hope, that they know how you feel and what your values are is risky.

Your adolescent will be extremely lucky to have a great sex ed class and teacher in school. Absent that, they will learn from their peers and porn. A 2022 survey by commonsensemedia.org found that 73 percent of teens seventeen and younger have watched porn, and 54 percent of kids thirteen and younger have seen it.[29] This isn't the *Playboy* magazines from the '80s. Assume that the majority of what they're seeing is misogynistic, violent, lacking consent, and teaching them intimacy as an act of personal fulfill-ment that uses others as accessories to help them reach that goal.

This obviously hurts girls and young women, but it also hurts boys. A lot of teen boys I've talked to have shared secrets about body image issues, anxiety about being able to get or keep an erection, and insecurity about their sexual performance with a real person.

Lack of Accurate Information Means More Harm

Many thoughtful boys and young men I've spoken with have admitted to engaging in nonconsensual sexual acts with girls. These boys are flooded with shame, wondering if they're sex offenders or predators. Many of them had lost all their friends and been obliterated on social media, even in cases when the behavior was in question. These young men absolutely need to be held accountable and are typically responsible. But in some ways, they've been set up to fail. The lack of honest emotional and sexual education and conversations from healthy adults creates a void filled by porn and a culture with modeling that says men are superior and entitled. Sadly, we just haven't made enough progress in the way we support our boys. It's never too soon to start teaching our kids about boundaries and consent.

It's Not All Bad

Relationships during middle and late adolescence can also be extremely beneficial. They provide opportunities to practice emotional "adulting": managing differences and conflict, solving problems, expressing emotions, sorting out gender and sexual identity. In most cases, both partners are happy and enjoy one another.

The average length of a relationship during adolescence is six months. There's a good chance you will disapprove of the person your child dates. You will most likely be uncomfortable with aspects of their relationship.

There will certainly be aspects that are unhealthy. There will be codependence. There will be breakups and getting back together.

It's important to accept that by middle adolescence (phase 2), for many teens their relationships will involve exploring their sexuality. This may involve intercourse, but more often includes kissing and touching.

By middle adolescence, research shows that sexually active teens have no more difficulties than their counterparts who have delayed sexual activity.[30] The same cannot be said for phase 1, as early adolescents who engage in sexual activity are at significantly greater risk for other behavior problems over time. So instead of getting overly focused on whether your teen is having sex, I encourage you to prioritize getting them the right information about the emotional aspects of sex. It can be helpful to ask questions like "How would you know if you're emotionally ready? How would you determine if your partner is?" This also includes basic conversations about consent, meaning more than getting a partner to say "Sure," but actually hearing an enthusiastic "Yes, please!" Sharing solid information also includes talking about birth control: different options, what works, and how they work. The research is clear: focusing only on abstinence until marriage increases their risk of an unplanned pregnancy.[31]

Talking about the emotional aspects of sexual activity along with facts about safe practices doesn't mean you're saying "Please have sex right now; you have my blessing." The majority of early and middle adolescents who share with me say that they regret their first time, even if it was consensual, because they just weren't ready. Most teens would benefit from waiting a bit longer than their hormones—and the culture—might tell them.

It's good and important to share what your values and preferences are and why. Your teen is more likely to comply with your wishes and think twice in those tempting and awkward moments if they've been armed with accurate information along with skills to set and respect boundaries. Your curiosity and empathy for their unique experience and what they're going through will go a long way as well.

Breaking Up

This is the hardest part of romantic relationships for most teens, and it's often followed by a temporary bout of depression and decreased self-esteem. Some kids will be more sensitive to this than others, and of course, the one broken up with will suffer more than the one who did the breaking up. It's important to be very thoughtful during these situations. Avoid the platitudes— "Plenty of fish in the sea"; "Everything happens for a reason"; "She/he is no good, and I think you're better off." Apply the ACE of PACE: Accept what are often mixed feelings led by sadness, stay curious, and offer empathy. You and I know that with perspective, they'll look back on this as just a high school or college breakup, and they'll be fine. But while they're in it they often feel shattered. For many teens, the pain they feel is amplified by worries about their reputation or friendships going forward. Remember, social dynamics can be very complicated.

Fewer words and lots of connection—that's often what your teen needs when going through these hard times. Taking them out to eat, playing a video game together, or doing something else that interests them is often the best way to help them navigate the big feelings they are going through.

If your teen is the one doing the breaking up, they may need coaching on how to be respectful and thoughtful about their soon-to-be ex. For example, many teens need to learn why it's generally not a good idea to break up over text. These days, that's an all-too-common tactic for avoiding the conflict, sadness, or tension. Breakups are uncomfortable and stressful for both parties, so the desire to avoid is understandable. But it's important to help our teens learn to manage these moments thoughtfully and responsibly.

Model Healthy Relationships

Having a good relationship with your spouse or coparent, if you have one, and with friends and family is one of the most effective ways to teach your kids how to have healthy relationships. For better or worse, kids are observing us and learning from what we do and how we interact with others. Are you gossiping? Raging? Avoiding others? How do you let others treat you? None of us is perfect, but our relationships, or lack thereof, matter immensely and will color how our kids will act with their peers and eventually as adults.

If you're in a loveless, conflict-free, "we're just friends" marriage, consider the impact that might be having on your teen over time. Ask yourself: What is my teen learning about love from watching me? What are they learning about healthy emotional expression and connection? How are they impacted by the tension and nonverbal communication between the two of you? These are also great questions to ask your teen.

I see many married couples who are great parents but have neglected their relationship—and used the kids as an excuse. In many cases, the best parenting advice I have for these couples is to focus on their relationship. This often requires making a hard decision, to either recommit and invest in the marriage or make the important choice to end it in a respectful way that puts the kids first. Kids need parents who are happy and whole more than they need parents who are married.

Summary

Your teen's social world is a complex set of different types of relationships that you or I will never be fully privy too. This world likely exists both online and off. Our job is to respect their need for autonomy and privacy while also valuing the importance these friendships hold for them. When friendship dynamics are unhealthy, it can be really hard to stand on the sidelines and watch. Remember, the best way to positively influence the choices your teen makes is by strengthening and maintaining your own relationship with them.

As your child attempts to navigate this fluid and tenuous aspect of their life, it's important to be available and accepting. As we talked about in chapter 5, accepting doesn't mean you agree with their choices in friends or a partner, just that you get how important these people are to them.

The friends your teen has now may be there for life or may drift away next week. Your teen is learning so much from the experiences they have with others. They are learning how to be in the world, how to collaborate and problem solve. And if they haven't already, they will hopefully learn about heartbreak and get to experience the wisdom and maturity that follow it.

The ups and downs your teen goes through will likely be triggering for you at times. Resist the instinct to try to control this part of their life. They'll figure it out. Healthy or not, the relationships your child has right now will ultimately teach them something about themself. Most important, don't forget to enjoy the unbridled joy and enthusiasm that can be found only when a group of teens gets together to play.

CHAPTER 7

Other Adults: You Can't Do It Alone

Sarah was fourteen when she found out that her mom, Kristi, had breast cancer. She and her mom were tight. When her mom told her, Sarah was stunned. It was just the two of them, as she'd never known her dad, who'd left them when she was a baby. Sarah's instinct was to be strong. She was a high achiever and never had any interest in the drug or party culture. She loved science and wanted to be an engineer.

Kristi grew increasingly worried about Sarah, who never showed any emotions about her cancer diagnosis. When asked about it, Sarah would respond with some version of "I'm fine, and I know you'll be okay." She would be there for her mom when she could, but she mostly buried herself in school activities and her after-school job.

Kristi knew that Sarah was close with her grandmother Betty, Kristi's mother, who'd been like a second mother to her when she was growing up. Kristi called her mom and asked if Sarah could spend the weekend with her. And could Betty maybe even check in with Sarah about how she was doing? Betty was excited about the idea and immediately started texting with Sarah to make plans for a fun weekend together. Sarah was also looking forward to it, despite being a bit stressed about keeping caught up with her schoolwork.

Betty had a way about her that drew Sarah close. She was authentically nurturing and warm while still commanding respect and authority without having to wield it. Sarah found herself doing things for her grandma that she just wouldn't do at home. She volunteered to help with chores and even opened up about her feelings. With warmth and kindness in her eyes, Betty asked Sarah how she really felt about her mom's cancer diagnosis. Sarah's stoicism cracked. Her eyes welled up and her hands shook. Betty pulled her close. Sarah broke down, crying uncontrollably. After a few minutes of loud, hysterical sobs, Sarah became calm enough to share. She revealed her terror along with her exhaustion from expending so much energy blocking out her thoughts about what her mom was going through and the possibility of losing her. She couldn't imagine her life without her mom. Betty reassured Sarah that they would get through this together and that the diagnosis was unlikely to be terminal. But mostly she hugged and held her as Sarah's tears soaked through her sweater.

After that weekend, Betty and Sarah started a routine of texting every day. Usually with just mundane stuff, sometimes exchanging memes or interesting things about their days. Betty was a lifeline for Sarah as she navigated the ups and downs of her mom's cancer treatment. Betty provided a type of support that only another adult could provide.

Why Teens Need Other Adult Relationships

So far we've talked about why, even when our children are teens, our connection with them is foundational to their ability to self-regulate and build healthy relationships with themselves and others. Building on that foundation, they require peer relationships to learn more about themselves and their values and to further develop their long-term intimacy skills.

The third essential form of connection they need is other adult relationships (OARs).

Just as we need actual oars to navigate rough waters or to paddle upstream, our kids need OARs to help them navigate the turbulence of adolescence and early adulthood.

I often ask other parents, teachers, coaches, camp counselors, and other adults who have spent time with my kids the same type of question you probably ask: "How'd it go?" or "How'd they do?" The answer is almost always some version of "Great!" or "She was wonderful" or "He was helpful." They tell me that when there is a need for redirection, my kids listen well and make the required corrections to their behavior. In short, other adults love our kids.

The experience other adults have of our kids doesn't always match what we're seeing at home. At times I've found myself questioning the other adult's experience. "Are you sure? You can be honest; I won't take it personally." But I'm always met with assurance that all went well with my kids in my absence. I bet it's similar with your kids. If your teens stayed with us for the weekend, I'd likely have a positive report to pass on to you as well. This is due in part to the fact that kids do better with other adults—that is, adults other than their own parents.

It's not that it's easy for teens to behave well and difficult to behave poorly. It's the other way around. It takes a lot of effort and energy to focus and behave as they're expected to for others outside the family. They act like gremlins only when they've run out of bandwidth or just don't have the skills to hold it together anymore. From an evolutionary perspective, behaving well for those outside their own family makes sense. They're more likely to survive if they fail with their family than if they fail out in the world. They need to be more invested in succeeding in the wild, because they're going to be expected to be out there surviving on their own soon.

We Parents Can't Do It All

Some of the pressure and stress that comes with modern parenting has to do with an expectation that we have to do it all. We should be our kid's friend, teacher, parent, therapist, camp counselor, personal assistant, and coach. Oh, and we should be really good at these roles, or at least as good as those other parents on Facebook, who seem to be killing it.

Of course, we can't possibly do it all. And even if we could, our kids would be missing out on so much. When we leverage the relationships of other adults, our lives get easier, and our kids gain more connection, learn new skills, and build on skills they already have. Everyone wins.

This is how we evolved as a species. For most of human history, families lived in multigenerational communities, and kids were parented and mentored in how to survive by a variety of adults around them. Unfortunately, in our modern nuclear family culture many of us have lost this cooperative environment. It's easy to feel unsure that we can trust other adults with our kids, which only exacerbates our isolation.

While kids absolutely need a primary attachment figure (typically this is a parent), research and intuition tell us that kids do best when they have a secondary or other primary attachment person or people in their life.[32] This means that our kids need other adults in their life whom they experience as reliable, trustworthy, and caring. This could be a family member, a neighbor, another parent, a teacher, a coach, or even a therapist.

Why Are Other Adult Relationships So Beneficial?

Our degree of wellness or pain is rooted in our interpersonal relationships. For our children, this begins with their first breath in the world and continues from there. As babies they need to be held and attuned to. As toddlers, they need to be physically comforted; our facial expression and body language needs to mirror theirs, which helps them feel seen and soothed. We get excited about their art and share in their pride as they swing across the monkey bars. We send them to school not just for learning and academic achievement, but for social enrichment and connection as well. Here they learn about being part of a community. A good educational environment helps them strengthen self-regulation, empathy, and problem solving and build their self-esteem.

Our teens are in essence doing an internship in how to be adults. Part of this requires learning how to be in a community. As such, they need to navigate different styles of leadership, conflict, and dealing with unique personalities. They need to communicate their needs and wants effectively to others, to collaborate and work successfully with them. If we have any hope of changing our divisive society, our kids will need to learn to engage with people who have views different from their own. All of this requires lots of exposure to other adults.

Here are some of the many ways that OARs benefit our kids:

- Other adults facilitate our teens' transition to adulthood by helping them feel like they belong to the larger culture and world. OARs help our kids feel like they matter and have something real to contribute. When teens trust another adult, it often takes very little for that adult to make an impact. When my daughter's eighth-grade English teacher asked to use her essay as an example to share with future students, it strengthened her confidence as a writer in a way that our praise could never do.

- Other adult relationships help inoculate our kids from mental health issues and loneliness while enhancing their self-confidence and sense of belonging. There's a vast array of quality mentoring programs, like Friends of the Children and Boys & Girls Clubs. Organizations like these have solid data showing the positive impact that playful, caring, and reliable adults have in the lives of the youth they serve.

- Teens will often listen to OARs in a more open way than they will with the parental figures in their lives. As a therapist, I see this daily. Many things I say to my teen clients have been said to them by their parents with no impact, but hearing it from me resonates simply because I'm not their parent.

- Teens are often more likely to confide in an OAR. There are certain things that your teen just may not share with you no matter what. Providing them with another outlet is essential. Adults age eighteen and older can be especially powerful supports for teens. They're old enough to listen and offer good advice, but young enough to still seem cool. If your teen is lucky enough to have an older sibling, cousin, or family friend in their life, do your best to nurture this relationship.

- OARs offer adulting and appropriately risky experiences that we're not able or willing to provide. This could be that theater teacher who offers an important role in the play or the responsibility to manage the tech. The coach who promotes the teen to the starting unit. The uncle or aunt who takes the kids on an adventurous backpacking or river rafting trip.

- Religion also offers structured and important ways for teens to connect with adults. In Jewish tradition, we have bar and bat mitzvahs where twelve- or thirteen-year-olds work with a tutor and their rabbi to study a portion of the Torah and read from it. They spend nearly two years preparing for this. On the day of, they read this challenging text and give a talk to the congregation of a hundred or more people about what they've learned and how to be a good person in the world. These young people are always nervous, voice often cracking. They're also inspiring and officially embraced by the adult community in a way that they never have been before. It's a very empowering process.

- Other adults offer parents a much-needed mental break, allowing us essential opportunities to recharge and renew by ourselves or with others. OARs allow us to get more breaks and prioritize that elusive concept of self-care. Of course, finding time apart from our teens isn't the hard part; in fact, we typically want more time with them than they want with us. But just because we're physically apart doesn't mean there's emotional distance. Too many of us are consumed with worrying and ruminating about our kids when we're apart. We're monitoring their location, checking their grades online, wondering whom they're with and what they're doing. Having another trustworthy adult who is able and willing to spend time with your teen can make it easier to recharge emotionally and mentally. Accept this other adult's offer as a well-deserved opportunity for some psychological respite. Focus your attention on a hobby or interest. Think about other things. Reinvest in those important relationships that you've been neglecting.

- Other adults help prepare our kids for the adult world by exposing them to different personalities, opinions, and strengths. Some of us may be lucky enough to be able to provide our kids with everything they need materially. But none of us will be able to provide all of the necessary values, traits, and skills that they will need to become well-rounded adults. I'm sure you're a wonderful person, but you—like all of us!—also have blind spots, issues, and flaws. That's part of being human in this world.

- OARs also give us and our kids opportunities to learn about and practice healthy boundaries. For example, a young adult neighbor has a cool new video game system and invites your child over to play. What boundaries do you want to set to be comfortable with this invite? How do you want to check in and monitor to make sure it's a safe relationship? The vast majority of adults are safe and caring people. At the same time, we want kids to trust their instincts, set boundaries, and ask for help, as needed, concerning their time spent with other adults.

I'm naturally pretty good at being empathetic, understanding, and playful with kids, both my own and others. This makes it pretty easy for me to connect and build rapport. However, I can be a bit permissive or passive at times when it comes to boundaries and limits. As a result, I always appreciate it when my kids are exposed to OARs who are a bit tougher or more strict, even if they are a little rough around the edges.

We all have weaknesses to work on. The more awareness we have about our own shortcomings, the better our chances of balancing it out by exposing our kids to other adults that have complementary skills and traits. This is one reason having a job can be such a great experience for a teen.

The Benefits of a Job

My first job was at my neighborhood Burger King when I was fifteen. This was so exciting to me. My parents had to take me shopping to pick out the required black shoes to go with my navy blue pants, collared shirt, and blue cap. I was so nervous and afraid of screwing up. My first responsibility was learning the fry station. Dump the bag of frozen fries into the basket, insert the basket into the fryer, push the third button, take them out, let them drip, dump them into the tray under the heat lamp, and add salt. I was working hard, uncertain how I was doing, until my manager came up and said, "Are you sure you've never done this before? You're doing great." That was all I needed to hear, and it's interesting that I still remember that. I also learned how to sweep and mop and other cleaning skills that I'd never learned at home. I interacted with customers who were as old as my grandparents. I'll never forget the first check I ever received: It was for $32, and it was amazing. (I also faced the reality of tax withholding, which was a different kind of amazing.)

Most teens benefit from having a job. They learn to manage stress and time along with the importance of following instructions and collaborating with others. Occasionally they get lucky and experience a boss who truly cares about them as a person and takes an interest in their success.

It's important to acknowledge that many teens *have* to work in order to help their families. For these teens, working isn't about personal development or extra money for boba tea. They are typically already caring for siblings and even parents, taking on responsibilities far beyond their developmental capacities. Many of these teens are forced to relate to adults as peers, not as mentors or guides who support and care for them. It's true that most of these kids grow up extremely mature and tend to take on too much responsibility in relationships. But they also sometimes struggle with allowing themselves to play, relax, and receive support and care from others. For those children who have to grow up quickly and step into a more responsible role within their family, OARs are especially important in offering support, encouragement, and making sure that they feel seen.

The more opportunities our kids have to engage with other trusted adults, the better. At the same time, this also means a greater likelihood that they will also be exposed to behavior and attitudes that aren't aligned with your values.

When the OARs Fail Our Kids

Part of me would like you to think that I always say the right things and never accidentally say something hurtful or offensive to a client. But I want to be honest. I occasionally mess up, and I feel sad and embarrassed when I do. Here's one story.

I was working with a teen client—I'll call him Jack. Jack was on the quiet side, and I was doing my best to engage with him, to no avail. I knew that he was quiet, in part, because he felt overwhelmed and scared. He was firmly in shutdown. I abandoned my skills; in my frustration, I became activated and impatient. I tried to get him to talk more by putting a bit of pressure on him. I told him that if he wanted to get better, he would have to make more effort. It was toward the end of the session, and I could see him shutting down further. It was clear that he just wanted to leave. We ended the session, and he left my office. I was well aware that I had failed him.

The next day I spoke with his parents. They said Jack was really uncomfortable and didn't want to come back. I understood why. I explained a bit about what I thought might have happened and asked if they could get him to come back for just a thirty-minute appointment so I could at least apologize and end our relationship on a positive note. They got him to agree to this.

When I saw Jack the next week, I started by asking him how he thought it had gone in the last session. I knew he would be reluctant to be honest, because a lot of kids are conditioned to tell adults what they want to hear rather than risk getting into trouble of some sort. I reassured him that I'd really love his honesty. I took the lead by stating what I thought his experience might have been: "Last week didn't seem to go very well. I don't think I did a very good job of listening. I can see how you might have felt judged for being quiet. I'm sorry for saying that it seemed like you weren't trying. I could see how that would be pretty hurtful and not even true. I actually think you were doing your best. I was the one who was not doing their job well."

Jack didn't have much to say, but he nodded and said he agreed. He did tell me that he didn't like me that much. That stung, but I understood that I'd blown it. My primary goal in this session was to show humility and model an adult taking full responsibility for the mistakes they'd made. He ended up working with another therapist, and I didn't expect to see Jack again.

OARs will fail your child. It happens, and I would put these situations in two general categories. The first involves adults who cross lines that cause trauma and harm in lasting ways. In those cases, we need to remove our kids from the situation and get them help and treatment. Hopefully, the offending adult is also held accountable. The much more common scenario involves adults who make mistakes or contribute to a misunderstanding that is hurtful to a child. All of our kids have experienced—or will experience—this scenario at some point.

Most of us, at one time or another, have had our kids come home to report that a teacher, coach, parent, or other adult said or did something that wasn't okay. Sometimes our kids' reports are accurate; other times, partially accurate; and sometimes, not at all accurate. Well-meaning adults who care about our kids will nevertheless let them down or disappoint them. Too often, in these cases, I see parents squander an important opportunity to empower their kids and allow them to learn from the experience. Sometimes the parents instead vilify the offending adult and cut them off from having any contact with their child. In other cases, the parents don't want to offend the OAR or make them uncomfortable, so they do nothing.

These situations are critical opportunities for kids to practice having hard conversations with other adults, and they very much need your help to do so. They may need you to have an initial conversation with the OAR; they may need you to go along with them to the conversation and offer support or help them find their voice. Other times, they may just want to role play what to do in the future and then let it go. Parents may show up loud and strong in these situations or avoid them altogether. What your child needs is for you to model open communication, curiosity about the problem, and thoughtful problem solving.

I've seen this countless times in my therapy practice. A teen has had a bad experience with a teacher, a coach, or even a family member, yet there was never an attempt to repair things with that adult. Sometimes in my conversations with teens, that offending adult is their parent. Unless I have reason to believe that it wouldn't be safe physically or emotionally to do so, I always recommend a face-to-face conversation with the parent or the other adult to talk about what happened. When a teen takes the advice and initiates a conversation, even if the outcome is simply to agree to disagree, the experience of building empathy, conflict resolution skills, and stress tolerance is invaluable. Remember, if your teen feels connected with and loved by you, they're more likely to be empowered, not derailed, by exposure to someone with a different point of view.

If you are the OAR in another child's life and you mess up (and we all do), think of it as an opportunity to model listening to the teen, offering a sincere apology, and making a plan to move forward. Do your best to approach the situation with openness and curiosity. In doing so, you will have a huge positive impact on that child's ability to be accountable and talk through hard things. When we don't help our teens initiate these face-to-face conversations with other adults, it only increases the hurt to our kids.

Barring rare exceptions, assume that the adults in your child's life genuinely care about them. When your child comes home and reports that another adult did or said something that wasn't okay, validate your child's experience, but also consider that there's likely more to the story. As parents, we've all had regrettable moments with our kids that, if taken out of context and isolated on their own, would reflect extremely poorly on us and be viewed by others as unacceptable.

When things go wrong between your child and another adult, whenever possible give your child the opportunity to meet with that adult to clarify and make things right. Through this process, they'll get to practice the urgent skills of communication and problem solving that our divided society desperately needs.

Many of our kids are drowning in a superficial online world of relationships. Many of us succumb to that, too. As parents, we have to model the importance of humanizing others and giving our kids opportunities to meet with other adults up close, especially when there are differences.

So, an important way to inoculate our kids from the toxic aspects of our culture is to support and nurture their relationships with other trusted adults. If a teen is struggling with mental health issues, even just one of these relationships could literally save their life.

Supporting Your Child's Relationship with Another Trusted Adult

- Ask adults your teen trusts if they'd be willing to reach out to your child and offer to spend some time with them.

- Schedule more time getting together with those family members your teen connects with.

- Let the other adult(s) know that your child really looks forward to and values time with them. Many of us don't realize the significance of our role or the impact we have.

- Provided that it's not a physically or emotionally unsafe situation, when there's an issue or dispute with an OAR, empower your child to work it out directly with that person. Start by assuming good intent. Help them, but don't do it for them. They might need your support by having you present or having you facilitate the conversation, but give them the opportunity to do as much of the process on their own as they are able.

- Process with your child afterward. Admit that sometimes adults do let kids down. Maybe their coach lost their temper and yelled inappropriately, and when your child tried to talk to them, they showed up defensive and closed off. In these situations your teen needs help thinking through how they can best continue working respectfully with the coach, whether they want to continue playing for them, and how it feels to have to work with an adult who is not receptive to feedback.

- When you see your teen talking with another adult, give them space to navigate that relationship. Nothing shuts down a conversation like parents coming over and getting involved. Later, you might offer to arrange a follow-up get-together for the two of them.

- Keep trying. Today many teens and families are more isolated from others than ever before. While some kids are lucky enough to have lots of other caring adults in their lives, many don't. It's easy for parents to feel isolated and then guilty that their child doesn't have more community. You may find that once you start thinking about the importance of OARs, you start to notice adults at school or in your extended family or community who care about your child and are happy to offer them a little extra support if needed.

- Talk about celebrities and influencers your teen admires. Do you remember that famous 1993 Nike ad where Charles Barkley states, "I am not a role model; parents should be role models.... Just because I can dunk a basketball doesn't mean I should raise your kids." This ad was very controversial; I think it sparked a good conversation. Teens are influenced by adults they admire in the community.

Teens are increasingly looking outside their immediate family for cues and perspectives about how to be in the world. Celebrities aren't all like Barkley; those who act like jackasses aren't responsible for our kids' behavior, but they are in a position to help, and they often squander it, making our job that much harder. So have conversations with your teen about the celebrities they look up to. Ask them which of their qualities they admire. This is a great opportunity to acknowledge the complexities of individuals and our feelings about them. Remember to focus on acceptance and curiosity so your teen doesn't shut down.

While we all have aspects of our parenting where we can continue to improve, sometimes the stress and frustration we're feeling is a result of trying to do it all on our own. If you're like me, asking for help is hard. Sometimes it feels like we're absolving ourselves of responsibility. Many of us view asking for help as a sign of weakness. But we have to rethink this. For more than two hundred thousand years, human children have been raised by communities. We're not supposed to be doing this all by ourselves.

Supportive adults offer a form of guidance, wisdom, and support that neither your teen's friends nor you can provide in the same way. Find individual adults in your community whom your child will be naturally drawn to, and do your best to nurture those relationships. These can be anyone from family members to even paid mentors. The more trustworthy and caring adults your teen has in their life, the better chance they'll have at becoming successful adults themselves over time.

PART III

Correction After They Blow It

You now know that connection is foundational to your adolescent's mental health—and it requires continual investment. Now comes the part that you may be champing at the bit for. Perhaps you're thinking, *Okay, connection is good, but my kid is still making poor choices. What do I do? I love them, but I also want to kill them. Can I give them consequences for poor behavior?*

Yes...no...well, maybe.

When it comes to what effective parenting means, there actually is hard science that is both consistent and clear.[33] There are two general qualities that lead to the best outcomes in kids. The first is a high level of warmth and connection. That's what the bulk of this book has been about so far. The second is a bit trickier: It's high expectations and reasonable consequences. So: Lots of warm connection. Lots of high expectations.

This part of the book will take you the rest of the way to becoming the best parent you can be for your teen, and ensuring an enduring connection that can weather every storm in these turbulent years.

Consequences are an important component of growth and learning for kids. But this notion desperately needs clarifying. Too often, we conflate consequences with punishment as a method of deterrence. If we're honest, we may want them to suffer just a bit, so they'll think twice next time. However, on the receiving end of a punishment, kids often feel ashamed, angry, or resentful. Their modified behavior becomes about not getting caught rather than learning any lessons or gaining maturity.

The game of consequences as punishment is one we will win as long as we have the power. Over time, as teens get older, the power dynamic shifts, and they end up "winning" because we no longer have the upper hand.

Of course, no one really wins. In a family, we sink or swim as one.

We often fall short in doling out consequences because we lose sight of why we're doing what we're doing. Often we're just too angry or defeated, so we react out of impulse or desperation. Too many kids are simply too harshly punished. Or the pendulum may swing all the way to the opposite end of the spectrum: zero accountability.

As the saying goes, an ounce of prevention is worth a pound of cure. My hope is that by following the strategies in this book, you will eventually find yourself needing to think about consequences very little, if at all.

The next two chapters will give you tools to make it less likely you will butt heads or experience unhealthy conflict with your teen. Chapter 8 will show you how to approach expectations in a way that contributes to more compliance and regulation in your household over time. Chapter 9 will show you how to respond, when your teen falls short of your expectations, in a way that teaches and builds their skills and confidence. Keeping the end in mind, we want our kids to become happy adults. Achieving happiness entails qualities like meaningful relationships, self-control, personal accountability, and emotional intelligence. This is not a quick fix, and it may require some uncomfortable changes on your part. But I hope that you will start to see the value of these strategies fairly quickly.

CHAPTER 8

Setting the Bar: Effective Expectations

Jeff was clearly fed up. "Toby treats this house like a hotel! He comes home from school, drops his stuff in the living room, walks into the kitchen looking for a snack, complains if there's nothing he likes, then promptly goes up to his room. On a good day, he might say, 'Hey.' He only seems to care about hanging out with his friends. Last weekend, for example, I asked him to be home on Saturday afternoon because I needed his help getting the house ready for some family coming to visit on Sunday. He said he would. But then he showed up around 4. At 5:30 he said he needed to leave again because he had a commitment that evening with some friends. I was furious. We got into a huge fight that night.

"The most frustrating part is that we actually have a good relationship. We do a lot of things together like camping, fishing, and cooking. I've really been making an effort to stay regulated and curious. We even play video games together, and it's fun! I feel like I do all those things you suggest when it comes to connection. I do think it's helped a lot, but I'm still super frustrated at his lack of consideration toward anyone else in the house. I'm ready to just take his phone and throw it off a cliff!"

Variations of this story and the exasperation that underpins it are common in my office.

When I met with Toby and his father, he had a slightly different take on it all. While he knew he could probably do more, he felt like he was doing a lot. He gave examples: Sometimes he did chores without being asked, he got decent grades, and he was almost always on time for family dinners.

I asked Toby for his perspective about what had happened on Saturday. Toby turned to his dad and said, "You said you needed me to be home on Saturday afternoon, so I took that to mean anytime before like 4 p.m. I meant to be home earlier, but I lost track of time and it took me longer to get home than I anticipated, which is definitely my fault. I also thought I would be done by 6, so I promised my friend that I would show up to her birthday party by 6:30." Toby clearly felt bad, but he wanted his dad to know that it wasn't because he didn't care.

I shared with them that I didn't think Jeff was being unreasonable in wanting Toby to spend a bit more time out of his room or in his request that Toby be home on Saturday afternoon. I also let Toby know that I didn't think he was ill intentioned, selfish, entitled, or anything like that. It seemed like Toby struggled with time management and accurately assessing how long things will actually take. I conveyed to Jeff that I didn't think taking away Toby's phone or grounding him would be necessary or helpful. I certainly scored points with Toby on that one.

Instead, I talked with them about expectations, and it turned things around.

What Are Your Expectations?

I'll come back to Toby and Jeff, but first let's back up and talk about why the question of consequences comes up in the first place. We consider consequences when our child has acted in a way that we deem inappropriate, unacceptable, or unsafe. They haven't met our expectations. But too often, our expectations are vague, inconsistent, or unrealistic—or we haven't even expressed them.

All of our kids will mess up, in ways small or big. Mistakes and poor judgment are necessary steps on the path to independence and adulthood. Our kids will lie about things like where they went, schoolwork, and chores. Too many teens today are chronically activated and/or shutdown. As you now know, in this state their ability to make sound decisions and consider the future is seriously hindered. When they're shutdown, they just don't care. When they're activated, they're more impulsive and often reckless.

In chapter 2, I talked about the often large gap between what our kids know and how they act. We may not be able to completely close that gap, but we can narrow it considerably by clarifying our expectations for them. Doing that will require more conversations and fewer assumptions.

Low expectations often result in kids losing their sense of agency and ultimately becoming more shutdown over time. Expectations that are inconsistent, confusing, or arbitrary often make kids more anxious and fearful. In contrast, effective expectations promote prosocial behavior and better judgment overall. So we need to clearly and consistently communicate our expectations and the values at the heart of each of them.

The most effective expectations are grounded in five essential qualities that I call the five C's: core values, clarity, consistency, capacity, and collaboration.

Core values. Adolescents are highly averse to rules or expectations that they perceive to be arbitrary or lacking in valid reason or logic. There's no better way to frustrate a teenager than to explain an expectation with "because I'm the adult, and I said so." Teens are much more willing to comply with expectations when they're grounded in core values. Examples of core values are adequate sleep, good mental health, quality family time, sufficient regular exercise, setting goals for the future, kindness, caring about others and your community, and healthy relationships. Core values are the foundational "why" of our requests.

It was helpful for Toby to hear his dad explain that he wanted him to bring his stuff upstairs after school because the family room was a shared community space that Jeff worked hard to keep reasonably clean, and he felt stressed when it got too messy. Jeff also talked about why Toby's helping out on that Saturday was more than just cleaning. In addition to wanting Toby to contribute to the family, he also was hoping to spend some quality time together in the process. Toby's behavior had come across like he didn't care about either.

Clarity. Many kids, especially young adolescents, are very concrete. When we explain what we're asking of them, it's important to make sure that they've heard us the way we intended. It can be helpful to confirm with a question like "Just so we're clear, what's your understanding of the expectation or agreement?"

Jeff learned that "be home in the afternoon" was unlikely to work with a kid like Toby, who often struggles with time management. Jeff agreed that in the future he would be more clear about a specific time he needed Toby home, and why. Jeff also clarified his request that when Toby comes home from school, in addition to taking his bag upstairs, he will check in briefly. Jeff also empathized with Toby's need to grab a snack and spend some time in his room to decompress after school. They discussed specific snacks that could be kept in the house as well.

Consistency. If you're really clear but don't follow through, then you'll lose a bit of credibility the next time around, and more conflict will ensue. It's important to be sure that you're able and willing to stick with your end of the agreement. For many of us, this is the hardest part, because it takes a lot of energy up front. We don't want to have to remind them, follow up, or stay on top of the situation with them. But this is exactly what we may need to do.

Jeff accepted that there would be times in the beginning when Toby might still leave his backpack on the living room floor and go right upstairs without checking in, both out of established habit. Jeff agreed to not take this personally and understood that he would likely need to remind Toby of this agreement. Toby said he would work on not getting defensive when his dad offered reminders.

Capacity. Sometimes your expectations are mismatched with your teen's capacity. For example, if they failed a class due to not turning in assignments, their behavior is telling you that they may not have the capacity to turn in assignments on time right now without more support. In this case, making them agree to turn in all their assignments on time next quarter—or else!—is a setup for failure and disappointment. In other cases, the expectations might be outdated, and they actually have the capacity for more.

Capacity is tricky, because the best expectations push the edges ever so slightly. But when we voice these, our kids predictably respond with resistance, insisting that they can't or it's too hard. They're experiencing the inherent stress that comes with growth. We're going to get this one wrong a lot, so we have to be flexible and adaptive. Perhaps the primary tool to help us calibrate their capacity with our expectations is our paying attention to their behavior. In contrast, when we measure our kid's capacity against other kids' or what they "should" be capable of for their age, we will often get it wrong.

Jeff thought about this and believed that with more clarity and consistency, Toby would have the capacity to follow through with these improved expectations.

Collaboration. As kids get older, we have to support their growing need for autonomy and control. Collaboration involves asking for their input and valuing their point of view. You have the final say as the parent, but it's important that your teen feels like they have a seat at the table when expectations are being established. The more your teen feels like they have input into the decisions being made, the more motivation they'll have to comply. Adolescents are smart; they know they need limits. They even want them.

But they also want, and deserve, to be treated like the budding adults that they are.

When Collaboration Isn't Possible

Sometimes there are difficult situations where kids aren't capable of collaborating with important decisions that will support their well-being. In these moments your teen's amygdala and nervous system will team up to create resistance. When they refuse to collaborate, it's still important to follow the other four C's. When they see that you are clear about the situation and intend to be consistent, initially their defenses will likely kick in. They may yell or make threats. You will need to stay calm and you may need support from others. Remember that they're responding from a place of fear and the need for survival. The more you're able to stay regulated and grounded in the core values behind your request, the sooner they'll recover and comply.

It's extremely difficult to see our kids distressed in any way. It's a biological instinct in these situations to want to make them feel better if we can. The most certain way to do that is to drop the expectation in these moments, because the peace and calm is instantly restored. But the cost, over time, is more anxiety and a constant need to walk on eggshells.

Let's consider another example.

Mary and Erin met with me to seek help with their son, Luke. The only thing he seemed interested in was playing video games. When he did join in family activities like dinner or a hike, he acted uninterested and participated at a bare minimum until he could get back to gaming. For a while, they ignored it and chalked it up to normal teen behavior. But after a few months, Mary noticed herself becoming increasingly irritated and concerned. This just didn't seem normal. He wasn't getting a lot of sleep, all his friends seemed to be online, and he wasn't very engaged in other areas of his life. As he became increasingly irritable, his parents were at their wits' end.

I asked them to evaluate their expectations when it came to video games. They both acknowledged that they were inconsistent and unclear about many of the rules. They had a rule that Luke needed to be off his game console by 10 p.m., but he regularly violated that without repercussions. He would join the family for dinner, but his game play would typically make him late. He would then scarf his food down and head back upstairs.

I helped them reevaluate their expectations by going through the five C's.

First, I asked them to explain their "why." Were they just managing their own anxiety? Were they out-of-touch, antigaming curmudgeons? Were they reacting out of anger, eager to punish? Or were their rules based on specific values?

They recognized that the need for new gaming restrictions was grounded in their *core family values* of health and wellness, including healthy sleep habits and more in-person quality time with family and friends. This foundational "why" for making changes helped them feel less guilty and fearful of Luke's negative reaction, because they knew they were doing the right thing for the right reasons.

Next, they got *clear* about a preliminary plan that felt reasonable to them:

- Console needs to be off by 10 p.m.

- No gaming until homework and chores are done after school.

- Show up to dinner on time and stay for at least fifteen minutes.

- Help clear the table and load the dishwasher after dinner before gaming can ensue.

- One hour of gaming per day on school days. Weekends and nonschool days, two hours of gaming per day.

Then they had to consider whether Luke had the capacity for these new expectations right now. As they thought it through, they accepted that at first he would likely do a poor job of clearing the table and loading the dishwasher, so they would be patient and provide support and encouragement.

Next, Mary and Erin had to consider whether they were able and willing to follow up with this and remain *consistent*. It was unlikely that initially Luke would stick with any change on his own. They exchanged a determined glance and recognized that, while it would be more work and time consuming in the short term, they were committed to following through and staying *consistent*. They were willing to absorb the short-term pushback in the service of doing the right thing and making things easier over time.

Finally, they made an effort to *collaborate* with Luke. They planned to sit down to talk with him about this new structure at a time and place where they could all be regulated. They started the conversation by emphasizing that he wasn't in trouble, and that they weren't mad. They were just concerned that his level of gaming was negatively impacting their time together as a family, his sleep habits, and his life offline in general.

Luke responded by thanking them and expressing gratitude for their love and support—

Just kidding! I'm not a fantasy fiction writer. That didn't happen at all. Luke couldn't have been more uncomfortable. It took everything in him to stay in the room and participate in the conversation instead of storming off or shutting down. Luke was able to settle a bit when his parents calmly asked him to share his feelings about their concerns. Of course, Luke didn't like this change, and he felt it was unnecessary, but he understood their concerns. Deep down, Luke knew his parents had a point.

The next step was discussing the new expectations. Mary and Erin shared their thoughts and asked Luke to offer his own ideas.

Luke felt that his parents' new plan was too restrictive, given how much he was used to playing. Erin asked him what he felt a reasonable amount of time was, and Luke came up with ninety minutes on school days once he got his chores and homework done, and three hours a day on weekends. Erin expressed concern that this would be too much time and that he would have a hard time stopping when his time was up. But because she was committed to supporting his autonomy and empowering his willingness to collaborate, they agreed to give this new approach a try.

While no one was thrilled at the end of this conversation, there was an odd mix of relief and anxiety among them all. Luke knew he was gaming too much and not being very nice to his family, although he wasn't convinced that the two were related. Luke also didn't trust that his parents would follow through on the agreements, which left him feeling a bit skeptical.

Mary and Erin were proud of themselves for having a calm conversation with Luke and relieved that he hadn't blown up at them.

When I saw Mary and Erin two weeks later, they reported that things were better overall. The first few days were tough, as Luke felt frustrated because he had to end his gaming after ninety minutes. Mary and Erin remained calm but firm and held him to it. By the end of the first week, once Luke saw that they were being consistent, he became much more agreeable and compliant. They described Luke as being more engaged with the family at dinner and overall. They attributed this to the fact that gaming just wasn't an option all the time, because the boundaries were clear.

Consider your expectations of your child. Do you need to ask more of them in some areas? Are you asking too much in others? Make a list. Put yourself in the shoes of your teen. Do they get the "why" behind your expectations? Are your expectations clear? Do they have the capacity for this right now, or do you need to start smaller? Does your teen experience you as consistent? As much as possible, do they feel included and involved in setting and following the rules?

Here are some additional considerations:

- Do you feel overwhelmed by a potentially long list of expectations? I know I can think of ten things right now that I would like my kids to start doing. It's important to triage. Sometimes we have to let things we care about go temporarily, because we have bigger fish to fry. If you're going through a particularly hard time with your child, your short list may not include having them clean their room, get good grades, or curb their screen time. Perhaps you need to start with safe behavior or getting to school. Start with one new expectation this week.

- "I just expect my teen to do their best" is a common sentiment that can be problematic for a couple of reasons. It's very difficult to measure effort. Our effort is going to look different depending on the state of our nervous system. An otherwise healthy and strong teenager who's struggling on the bottom rungs of their ladder and dealing with depression may be exerting a lot of effort just to take a shower or a walk around the block or sit through a family meal. This is one reason PACE can be so helpful. It allows us to more accurately assess what effort looks like in any given moment for our teen. It makes it possible for us to meet them where they actually are instead of where we wish they were or think they should be, and to move forward from there.

- If your child isn't able or willing to collaborate, do your best to involve them. Then let them know that you'll be making a unilateral decision without their input. In this case, a primary goal is to help your child learn to get better at having collaborative conversations. While this will certainly test your patience, hopefully you now know why there's no need to be mad at them for not collaborating, because they don't have the capacity yet—either they don't have the skills, or they're too activated or shutdown. When they predictably resist, you'll need to remind yourself that the expectation you're maintaining is the most loving thing you can do for your child right now. The rewards will come later.

- Have uncomfortable conversations. We need to talk about expectations regarding all of the things that make us uneasy, such as sex, racism, drugs and alcohol, suicidal thoughts, self-harm, anxiety, and depression. "Don't do it" or "You can always talk to me" are fine starting points, but not enough to begin making a change. What are the expectations if your teen does decide to have sex, or to use drugs or alcohol? What do you expect of them if they have suicidal thoughts or cut? What if they say something that's cruel or demeaning to another person? I know these can be difficult things to think about and daunting to talk about. In many cases, you'll need to get more informed on some of these topics. We ask our kids to do a lot of hard and uncomfortable things, and we need to do the same.

Expectations are hard because they induce stress for the recipient. When we set an expectation of our teen, they will often drop a couple of rungs down on their ladder, especially if it's new. This is okay; we're less concerned about where they are on the ladder and more interested in their ability to recover in healthy ways. When your teen rises to meet the request, they get to experience the rewards. The first is more self-esteem, confidence, and connection with you. The second is more resilience overall. In chapter 3 I shared that a resilient person has a flexible nervous system. The ability to drop down and then recover back to regulation is the foundation of a resilient person. Every time your teen gets to drop down and then recover is an experience of practicing resilience. Expectations are an important pathway to help them do that.

We don't need them to agree or comply or smile. Setting effective expectations requires us to be reflective and confident, and to know our child and what their capacity is now. Sometimes we have to start small.

None of us is perfect at this. Many of us aren't very good at it. That's okay. I am regularly inconsistent and lacking in clarity. I initially told my daughter that her weekly allowance would be tied to her completing specific chores each week. Week one went swimmingly. Then her chores got increasingly spotty, but her allowance stayed the same. After a few months, I tried to backtrack and tell her why I needed her to do more chores to keep her allowance, and it did not go well. Whoops. I need to work on this one. Fortunately, because I place such a strong emphasis on connection with her, I have a lot more wiggle room for error.

The goal here is improvement, not perfection. I know that when I am using more of the five C's, things just go better with my kids. The families I work with also consistently report having less conflict, more cooperation, and much less of a need for consequences when they use the five C's.

The fact is, despite our best efforts, our kids will violate our expectations and break rules. Then what? When expectations aren't met, there must be accountability—the focus of the next chapter.

CHAPTER 9

When They Blow It: Can I Punish Them or Do They Just Get a Hug?

As a teenager, I was generally what others would consider a "good kid." I never got in trouble, I didn't drink or smoke weed, and I did fine in school. I even secretly looked down on the "bad kids." In reality, I had an unaddressed anxiety disorder. I internalized everything. My lack of risk-taking was mostly driven by fear, not by some moral or ethical maturity.

I was sixteen when I went to my first real party. My best friend's older brother was nineteen and lived in a house downtown with friends. I knew there would be a lot of alcohol there, but I wasn't planning to drink. While I wasn't directly peer pressured, I was certainly peer influenced. My social anxiety and insecurity gave way to an easy and obvious solution in front of me: Absolut Citron and Malibu rum. So I chose to drink a little bit, then a little more. By the end of the night, I was swallowing anything I could find straight out of the bottle, all the while pronouncing to all who could hear that "I'm not drunk!" People seemed to think I was hilarious. Whether they were laughing at me or with me, I'll never know. By 1 a.m., I was vomiting in the bathroom. The next morning, I felt like an idiot and was embarrassed. It was clear that I was a source of entertainment to others, but I certainly didn't gain any respect that night.

A couple of days later, I told my dad what had happened. In return, he pronounced that I was grounded, he was going to take my car away for the weekend, and I wasn't allowed to go to that party house again.

That was it.

I was livid. I focused my powerless energy on how I could make him share in my misery. In my attempt at punishing him back, I ignored him and vowed not to talk to him all weekend.

On the surface, the consequence my dad gave me sounds reasonable. But consider this as well: I had never done anything like that before, and I had no interest in drinking again anytime soon. There were also some real natural consequences that I had experienced. It's also important to think about why I chose to drink in the first place. I had a hard time making friends, I wanted to fit in, and I had low self-esteem. Had I been met with empathy, listening, and an attempt to understand, many of these factors might have surfaced. Instead, I learned to be sneakier and to avoid being that honest with my parents in the future.

My parents weren't abnormal or bad. Back then, there was very little science or guidance about parenting. Most parents either did what their parents had done, or if that hadn't worked well, the exact opposite. Many of us have reacted to our kids' confessions in a fashion much like my dad's reaction. When our kids' behavior falls short of our expectations, we may respond by only half-listening at best and mostly with a lecture and punishment. We tend to see their explanations that they consider valid and authentic as just making excuses or justifying. This leaves our kids with two options: (1) put their head down and acquiesce, while silently seething, or (2) rebel with anger. Either way, the opportunity for learning and building empathy are missed while the connection that we've been coveting so much is further frayed.

In my own work with teens from all walks of life, I've never met a kid who didn't want to do well. No one truly wants to disappoint their parents. When they screw up, they feel bad, but they may not know how to do better or take responsibility without feeling shame, so they often act like they don't care. They may genuinely be lacking the skills to make a different decision or verbalize their needs. They know adults are frustrated with them, and over time, many teens start to hate themselves because they see the harm they're causing but can't find a way out. Sometimes they give up and decide that they aren't good enough, and their behavior becomes proof of the self-image they've created.

As we discussed in chapter 3, our nervous system is designed to protect and keep us safe. Your teen's negative behaviors are survival strategies, however unproductive. I can't emphasize this too strongly. Your teen's defensiveness, anger, or apathy are armored parts protecting them from their vulnerability—specifically fear, sadness, or shame. Accessing these core emotions is a critical step on the path toward more self-regulation and better judgment. Accountability is an opportunity to cut through the armor, making space for learning and growth to flourish. But we have to take the shame out of the mix and remove our blinders. Punishments like grounding and taking privileges away for long periods of time seldom achieve that goal and often result in thicker armor. Punishment is not accountability.

Accountability is about restoring and strengthening the capacity for coregulation—whether the problem is something minor like being late, or more significant transgressions like lying, stealing, physical or emotional aggression, or destroying property. In small or large ways, the transgression causes harm to an individual or community. Accountability gives the offending person—in this case, your teen—an opportunity to heal and grow.

Thinking this way requires a paradigm shift for many of us. Most of us grew up with the notion of accountability as being synonymous with tough punishments. Kids need to learn their lessons, we tell ourselves. Grounding, taking away things they love, public shaming—many people even glorify beatings they got as a kid, telling themselves it helped them become tough and strong. Sometimes long lectures and yelling are mistaken for account-ability. All of these attempts fall short if your teen isn't learning how to do better or opening their hearts to be more compassionate toward others in the future. At best, there is behavior change born of fear, as the nervous system becomes more alert and protective than before.

True accountability is about helping your child learn from their mistakes and get better, not worse. Accountability is about restoring and even strengthening authentic, coregulated connection. From this place, new stories can be created.

I think of accountability as a three-step process, with each step building on the last. Step one is holding ourselves accountable. We've all let our teens down and caused harm in some way. If we're filled with excuses, avoidance, and defensiveness, then it's unrealistic to expect any more than that from our kids. They will simply learn to be polished and sophisticated in their ability to evade accountability, the same way it was modeled to them. If there are some ways that you've harmed your child in the past that you think may still impact them, and these have not been repaired yet, it's not too late. I encourage you to take accountability now. By modeling this yourself, you will be teaching your child how to take personal responsibility, show humility, and apologize sincerely without shame. This doesn't have to involve a major harm caused. I will regularly apologize to my daughter during random conversations when I've found myself cutting her off and being dismissive of her perspective. In moments like this, I see her getting increasingly frustrated and on her way to shutdown. I apologize and change my behavior, and we keep it moving with regulation.

The second step is holding our teens accountable—the focus of this chapter.

The third and final step reflects the ultimate goal: that our teens learn to hold themselves accountable as adults. We're doing all of this hard work because we want our kids to be the type of adults who can genuinely apologize for mistakes they make and do better going forward. We want them to be the type of person who doesn't make excuses or blame others for their behavior. And we want them to do the right thing, not because they're afraid of getting in trouble or because of what others will think of them, but simply because it's the right thing to do. Teens aren't generally good at holding themselves accountable yet. It's our job to help them get there.

Why Accountability Can Be So Hard

Accountability is a gift of love we offer our kids, but it feels really hard, even impossible sometimes. Only the lucky few of us received healthy accountability in the face of our mistakes growing up. Most of us were either punished, yelled at, or ignored (which often feels worse). Some of us learned to be really good and managed to sidestep mistakes and the shame that might follow. This usually leads to a graduate degree in perfectionism. Another challenge is the message of permissiveness that is infused in many aspects of our culture. Some of us have become afraid of making our kids distressed or angry. This causes us to avoid accountability altogether.

Before I explain how to hold our kids accountable, it's important to address the barriers so many of us experience—the most common reasons why we parents avoid accountability:

- *We're afraid of them.* If you have a teen who's bigger than you and volatile at times, this may be a real concern. Accountability causes stress, and some kids can get scary. Sometimes this is a legitimate concern, and your child may need to be in a specialized therapeutic placement. More often than not, though, your fear is about your own anxiety. Kids feed off our energy. When they experience us as afraid or anxious, it triggers their own amygdala's fight response. Inside a scary kid is a scared kid.

- *We feel bad or guilty.* Most of us have a hard time seeing our kids in pain, be it physical or emotional. We might see their fragility and worry that we're stunting their development. Other times, we place so much value on the connection that the risk of their being mad at us is too much to bear. Write me down for this one!

- *We're just tired.* Sometimes it's as simple as that. We're worn out and find it easier to just let it go and ignore the issue. This is my second go-to.

- *We're paralyzed with uncertainty.* There are rarely perfect answers. Sometimes we can become fearful of doing the wrong thing, and we end up doing nothing. It's okay to take time to think and even consult with another parent or friend before you respond. But always try to go back and respond, even if it's to simply say, "This is a tough one, and I'm not sure what to do."

- *We aren't paying attention.* Some of us are just too busy. Accountability can be time consuming, and many of us are in go mode so much that we miss a lot of what's going on. If you're personally dealing with addiction or untreated mental health issues, this could also explain why you're missing important behavioral concerns.

It's so easy to let the business of modern life and/or our own issues get in the way of holding our kids accountable. But when we ignore issues, resentment builds, and we end up reacting disproportionately. We have to put in the work to teach accountability frequently and consistently.

I trust that, like me, you're motivated to work through your own barriers so you can hold your child accountable more often. This may require specific parent coaching, individual therapy, a modified work or life schedule, or simply more self-care. Look for progress, not perfection.

Now it's time to start holding your child accountable.

Next time your teen comes up short of the desired expectations, use these three R's of accountability: regulate, relate, and reason. This framework is adapted from the work of Bruce Perry, the psychiatrist I mentioned in the introduction to part 2.[34]

The First R: Regulate

We've all reacted to our kids' behavior while dysregulated ourselves. We're pissed off, and we want them to suffer, too. We want to get their attention, so we threaten to take away whatever they care about the most (phone, anyone?). We never leave these situations proud of ourselves, and we harm the relationship in the process.

So before you do anything else, get calm. Take your own time-out if you need to. It's perfectly okay to say, "I'm not sure what to do right now, and I need some time to calm down and think about it" or "I'm really angry, and I need a break and some time to cool off."

Remember our chapter 3 discussion of the nervous system? Our kids can't learn if they're not regulated, and they can't get regulated if we're not regulated.

This is extremely difficult, and sometimes nearly impossible to do in the moment. Often your child will try to keep you engaged. They'll follow you or say the most hurtful or offensive thing they can think of. So I strongly urge you to be preventative about it. The importance of self-care can't be overstated. We can often anticipate when the hard moments are going to come—their negative response when we set an expectation or enforce a consequence. So plan and prepare in advance. Clear your schedule if you have to, eat some Wheaties, and take slow, deep breaths before you lean into the moment.

The Second R: Relate

When our kids mess up, they're anticipating being in trouble. They may expect us to be mad or yell. Even if this couldn't be further from reality, and you're calm as a cucumber, your child's nervous system and amygdala are likely telling them a different story. They're bracing themself, so they will likely have their armor on for protection. Remember, they need this armor at first because they haven't learned to trust that you'll remain calm and are there to help.

Now that you're calm (you're still calm, right?), you can counter their defense by modeling that you're interested in hearing their side of the story. As you demonstrate with your words and body language that they're not in trouble, you're not angry, and you just want to have a conversation, you might notice that their body language starts to shift and settle a bit.

The Third R: Reason

Typically, when there's been a hard moment of conflict, there's a period shortly afterward when your teen will be more open to listen and dialogue with you.

Even healthy conflict can be so draining, but it's also a necessary and vital aspect of any relationship with teens. The brief period afterward is also an ideal time to repair the temporary frays in your relationship.

Even though you're likely to have their ear during these moments, don't overdo it by talking too much or making it all about you.

This is where learning happens. Sometimes a look or a few words are all that's needed to get the point across. Often a conversation is called for and nothing else is needed.

Please take this to heart: Their uncharacteristic actions that led to this conversation don't reflect all that they are as a person, nor are they an indictment of you as a parent. If you think there's something wrong with your teen, they'll feel that energy and will shut down. If you make it about yourself, by taking it personally or thinking they were disrespecting you, you'll miss the opportunity to help them take accountability. None of this is personal.

Listen and try to understand their perspective first. Then remember to expect that they'll hear you out as well. It has to work both ways. If they're still having a hard time with not getting defensive, you might say, "Please just consider what I'm saying." If they storm off or still can't get regulated, it just means that they're not ready yet. Let them walk away, but plan to follow up. Don't let them avoid the conversation altogether. Keep following up until a good-enough conversation happens. It doesn't have to be perfect. In these situations, good enough is great. It shows you care enough to keep trying and know that it's really important to work through what happened.

When having a conversation, focus less on information (I know that's hard; I love lectures) and more on fostering reflection and thoughtfulness. Sometimes you can just ask simple questions, like

- "What's your plan to get back on track at school?"

- "What's something you think *I* could work on? How about you?"

- "How can you determine when TikTok isn't fun anymore and is causing you more anxiety?"

Other times, it can help to mirror what you think they might be going through and share your own feelings. But keep it current and relevant; for example:

- "I can understand why you may have made that choice. Let me know if I have it right…"

- "You seem really angry."

- "Clearly, we're both really sad [hurt, angry, and so on]."

The final step of reasoning involves follow-up and action. It's essential that this step comes last. The most common mistake is attempting this too soon, when they're not ready.

This part of the conversation is a focus on going forward. Sometimes a good talk is adequate, but often you'll need to follow it with a tangible behavioral or structural change.

First, consider what skill deficits are getting them into trouble. Examples might include:

- Empathy/seeing another's point of view

- Self/impulse control

- Problem solving

- All-or-nothing thinking

- Expressing thoughts and emotions

- Emotional regulation

- Social skills

- Time management

You might look at that list and think, *All of them!* Be specific. There are areas your child struggles with more than others; focus on those.

Once you determine the trouble areas, consider a response that will support them in each area: natural consequences, repairs, and/or modified expectations.

Natural Consequences

If I don't pay my credit card on time, I have to pay a fee. Showing up late for work consistently will lead to being fired; speeding can result in an expensive ticket; mistreating others typically results in loneliness and painful relationships. Didn't bring a coat in winter? Expect to get cold. Didn't study for a test, or ignored an assignment? Expect to feel anxious and stressed. Treated a partner poorly? Expect them to leave eventually.

Natural consequences are an important part of life and how we learn. The goal here is to allow a real-world repercussion that simulates what they might experience as adults. This isn't about shaming or instilling fear or suffering as a form of deterrence. As a general rule, keep the time frame of consequences to within one or two days. Beyond that, the learning opportunity often fades and may get replaced with frustration and blind compliance. Examples of offenses and possible consequences:

- Stole money → Pay it back with interest.

- Graffiti → Spend a day cleaning graffiti in the community.

- Disrespecting a teacher → Apologize to that teacher in person (even if it's a terrible teacher; everyone deserves to be treated with respect).

- Stealing from a store → Meet with the manager, apologize, and pay them back.

- Sneaking use of a device → Lose use of it for all or part of the next day and/or write a report about healthy use of devices.

- Alcohol or drugs found in the car → Lose driving privileges for a time and/or clean and detail the car.

- Coming home past curfew → Come home early for a couple of nights.

Repairs

Ruptures are an inherent aspect of every relationship. There will be conflict. In fact, there should be. Many times, you'll be the one who misses the mark. For all my talk about empathy and curiosity, I've found myself on many occasions telling my kids to suck it up, push through, or just get over it. I sometimes have a tone and body language that's dismissive or even disgusted with their behavior. Sometimes Mariah and I will get into an argument and raise our voices while our kids are within earshot.

In our family, when someone crosses a line and makes a mistake that's hurtful to someone, we try to prioritize a repair. Repair is about reconnection and making things right. In struggling families, the core problem is never the conflict; it's the absence of understanding and repair. Hurt feelings go unaddressed. There's no acknowledgment or reconnection. Over time, this festers and produces anxiety, shutdown, even trauma.

What repair might look like:

- Taking personal responsibility for hurting the other, and offering a sincere apology

- Demonstrating empathy and some understanding of how the other was harmed or impacted

- Performing an act of kindness toward the person or people harmed

- Making a commitment to doing something different going forward

- Ending the conversation with physical and/or verbal affection and praise—hug it out and move on

Sometimes repairs are short and sweet, like a quick conversation. Other times, repair may be a process that occurs over days, weeks, or months. Repairing ruptures in your family is a powerful process and invites so much learning. Over time, you'll benefit from creating a culture of repair, and it'll be expected whenever things get out of hand.

Family life gets really messy sometimes. It's the price of caring deeply about others while living in a complex world. Over time and with practice, I think you'll find that prioritizing repair offers a beautiful opportunity for learning, reflection, and authentic connection.

Psychologist and best-selling author Rick Hanson put it beautifully: "A bid for repair is one of the sweetest and most vulnerable and important kinds of communication that humans offer each other. It says you value the relationship."[35]

Modified Expectations

In the last chapter we talked about how our expectations often don't line up with our kids' capacity. Your child's behavior communicates what they're capable of and ready for. In many cases, they're letting you know that they're not ready for certain freedoms and privileges. Sometimes we need to reevaluate and update our expectations in a way that sets our teen up for success, at least temporarily.

This can be a hard one, because it's always more difficult to pull back on expectations once norms have been established. Again, this is not about punishment or making them miserable, although it may feel this way to them. That's okay, because we're not trying to control their attitude or perceptions. We're just trying to do the right thing to help them learn, grow, and remain safe. To illustrate this purpose: An intersection next to my house didn't have any stop signs when we moved in. It was a block away from a very busy street that often got backed up. When traffic on the busy street backed up and someone got fed up, they would often turn onto this residential street with no stop sign and fly past all that traffic they'd been stuck in, often going 45 on a 25. It was dangerous. Stop signs were put in shortly thereafter, making the street much safer for everyone. Fortunately, no one had to be killed before changes were made.

Sometimes our kids just need some added stop signs because they've demonstrated that they aren't able to restrain themselves yet. It's important to clarify that this isn't a failure on their part or designed as a punishment. It's simply an attempt to help them reach the goals they've set for themselves. When framed in this way, many kids will let down their armor and agree, even if they're not happy about it.

When and Where

As I talked about in chapter 4, timing is important with teens. Typically, when you first confront their behavior, their initial response will be defensive. Expect this, and give them time to digest your desire to talk about what happened. This may take ten minutes, a few hours, or even a day. Then be willing to meet them on their home turf, which is often their room. Sometimes you may be able to have a chat in the car; other times it may work to gather in the living room or kitchen over food. The where is less important than the when. The key consideration is that you don't wait too long. There's a short window in which kids have an emotional connection to the mistake they made. During this time, they care and are motivated to make things better. Once that window closes, it's really difficult to get them to reconnect with that experience again.

Putting It Into Practice

Ben is a fifteen-year-old high school sophomore. He's a nice kid; shows up for family dinners and gets decent grades. During a routine Saturday afternoon laundry grab in Ben's room, his mom, Jackie, was shocked to find a bag of marijuana on his dresser and some empty liquor bottles sticking out from under his bed.

Her heart sank. Then she started to think about all the lies he'd clearly told her. She felt betrayed, hurt, and pissed off. She was ready to confront him, take away his phone for a week, and ground him for the weekend. He was out with friends and would be home in a couple of hours, which gave her some much-needed time to process this situation.

As Jackie was able to settle her nervous system, she moved from anger to sadness, and she started to cry and blame herself. How did I fail? What did I miss? What did I do wrong? Then she flashed to her brother, who had struggled with a drug problem for many years, and she started to get panicked again. Jackie knew that just grounding Ben and taking away his phone might provide some temporary catharsis for her while giving her a sense of control. But she also understood deep down that this wasn't going to address the underlying issues. She really wasn't sure what to do.

She reminded herself to regulate, relate, and reason.

First, she focused on getting calm by maintaining perspective. Ben is still a good kid, she reminded herself. He's likely going through some hard things, like shame and guilt. He needs support—not judgment and anger.

Now that Jackie was feeling more regulated, she focused on relating to Ben. She decided that when he got home, she would try to listen to his perspective while staying curious and loving.

Finally, Jackie also knew that there would have to be some changes. While there were still so many things going well, there were also clearly some things that weren't. She just wouldn't know what changes were needed until she understood more about what was going on with him. She was also hoping that she could get him on board with whatever was decided.

Here's how the conversation went when Ben got home:

Jackie: [*starting with connection*] Hey, how was the skate park?

Ben: [*offering little*] Fine.

Jackie: [*sitting on the living room couch with knots in her stomach*] We need to have a conversation. Have a seat.

Ben: [*now nervous but hasn't connected the dots yet*] Okay?

Jackie: I was doing laundry and went into your room to grab clothes off your floor, and I found a bag of marijuana and three empty White Claw bottles.

Ben: [*predictably activated and defensive*] Those weren't mine! What were you doing in my room anyways?

Jackie: [*working hard to stay calm*] I was literally just trying to grab some clothes to help you out with some laundry. I wasn't snooping. I had no reason to think you were doing any of those things.

Ben: [*reading Jackie's body language and seeing her being calm and kind, dropping his defenses*] Okay, well what do you want me to say? You're gonna take my phone and I'm probably grounded, right?

Jackie: [*kindly, warmly*] It's not about that. I don't want your phone. I just want to understand and figure out how to move forward. You're not a bad kid, and I don't think any less of you. If you're struggling, let's figure it out. Trust was broken, and I want to repair it.

Ben could feel his mom's empathy, care, and concern, which brought him more regulation. It took every ounce of his energy to not break down and cry.

Jackie: [*continuing to stay curious*] How often have you been drinking and smoking?

Ben: I started at the beginning of the summer and gradually started doing it more and more.

Jackie: Why do you think you do it?

Ben: Different reasons. It used to be kind of fun. A lot of my friends smoke, and they don't pressure me, but it's hard to hang out with them and not do it. It also helps me feel less anxious and overwhelmed sometimes.

Jackie's curiosity led to more empathy. She thought, *Overwhelmed and anxious. My baby's been overwhelmed and anxious, and I had no idea.* She felt bad that she'd missed this. He'd seemed to be doing so well. He was busy but mostly seemed happy and fine.

Jackie: I'm so sorry to hear this, sweetie. I had no idea you've been feeling overwhelmed.

Ben couldn't hold back his emotions anymore, and he burst into tears, the flood of pent-up sadness and loneliness released. They hugged and cried together.

Next, it was time for a reasonable response.

Jackie: Let's talk about expectations and moving forward so we can build trust back up. Do you have any thoughts about natural consequences or a repair?

Ben: No. What do you think?

Jackie: Well, I think it would be a good thing for you to start therapy so you can have someone to talk to other than me about your feelings and anxiety. It also might be useful for us to do some family therapy. Would you be open to that?

Ben: Sure.

Jackie: I'd also like you to deep clean your room and give me everything you have along those lines—bottles, drugs, paraphernalia, and anything else. I'm happy to help if you'd like.

Ben: Fine.

Jackie: Are you willing to abstain completely from weed and alcohol?

Ben: I don't think I can promise that. I'm just being honest.

Jackie: [*feeling stressed but staying calm*] Okay, thanks for being honest. That does concern me, because I think it makes you feel worse over time. Would you be willing to read an article, based in science, on the impact of marijuana on the adolescent brain? If you have something that you'd like me to read or watch, I'd be willing to do that as well.

Ben: Sure.

Things didn't end perfectly. Ben is sure to continue to struggle with managing his anxiety and will smoke weed at times, at least in the near future. But the value of Jackie's holding Ben accountable can't be overstated. Jackie demonstrated that she's someone that he can come to honestly without fear. Ben felt heard and seen, which provided enough regulation for him to be able to reflect on his choices and how they impact his mom. It gave him the safety to be vulnerable instead of shut down or defensive. Finally, some concrete and practical changes were made to help facilitate Ben's growth and development. There will be many more conversations like this. As they each get better at regulating, relating, and reasoning, the benefits to both of them, and especially to Ben, will be immense, and he will figure it out.

Conclusion:
Being Their Guide

The journey of parenting adolescents is a lot like a whitewater rafting trip. Mariah and I once rafted the White Salmon River in southern Washington. This four-hour trip culminated in a twelve-foot drop known as Husum Falls. This is one of the largest commercially rafted drops in the US. This plunge was dangerous enough that before getting in the rafts, we all had to get on a bus and drive to the bridge above and look down at the waterfall to ensure that we gave informed consent. The consent form said, in so many words, "I promise not to sue you if I die going down this waterfall, because you did warn me."

This trip was beautiful, as we rafted through a heavily forested gorge. We built rapport with our boatmates, including a few other parents and one pair of preteen siblings. Our guide, Dan, had a natural way of projecting confidence without seeming arrogant.

As much as I was enjoying the trip, I was feeling anxiety about the waterfall. If it's not clear already, I am not one to chase adrenaline, so this was a big step for me. As we got closer, I sought out reassurance from Dan. I half-jokingly asked him to guarantee that we wouldn't die. He said he couldn't guarantee that, but it was extremely unlikely that anything bad would happen. This qualified reassurance didn't help. He gave us instructions that if the boat flips and we fall in, to curl up into a ball and wait until you pop up to the surface. If you flail and panic under water, you'll sink deeper. So I made a mental note not to panic if I found myself in a situation where I could drown. Got it. No problem.

The moment of truth was upon us. There was a spot thirty yards short of the falls to pull over for anyone who wanted to get out and portage around the falls. Mariah and I looked at each other, considering the options. Part of me wanted her to ask to get out, so I'd have an excuse to follow along and "support her." We pulled over to the side, and the preteens got out. I wasn't about to be the only adult to exit at this point. So onward it was. Our guide gave us the signals to let us know when it would be time to get all the way into the raft and when to bring our oars in with us. These were two very important steps, he told us. I felt like my life was on the line. I looked at Mariah with a thin veneer of optimism to hide my fear.

We dropped down the falls and landed upright. No one fell out. I was so happy and mostly relieved. We high fived.

The journey of parenting adolescents is a lot like that trip. As much as we might want to control the outcome, the inherent uncertainty is both exciting and, at times, terrifying. It's beautiful and everything we hoped for, right up until it's not anything like we expected. We often spend too much time worrying about the end at the expense of enjoying the beauty right in front of us. If we flail and panic, we're more likely to get sucked under deeper. When we start sinking, staying calm and steady is the way back to the surface.

The monumental construction project happening in a teen's PFC, coupled with their frequently activated nervous system, makes teen behavior very inconsistent. Rushing whitewater rapids one moment, calm and peaceful waters the next. It's up to us to make sure they never feel like they're the only ones in the boat. Like the river guide, we need to project confidence and a steady hand to our teens, even if we're not feeling it inside. Building and maintaining a positive connection is a critical responsibility. This happens by our practicing an ongoing attitude of playfulness, acceptance, curiosity, and empathy. From there, it's our job to facilitate connection with the others in the boat—those healthy relationships with peers and other adults in the community. Finally, there must be expectations and accountability. The fun of our rafting trip came only in the context of expectations and agreements that were clear and consistently enforced and that everyone had the capacity to follow. We all held ourselves accountable, and we were even given the option of getting out if we felt like we weren't ready or able to meet the expectations.

Parenting our teens can feel like they're heading, unprepared, toward a twelve-foot waterfall. We have to trust in ourselves and in the support and community of others to make it through. No matter what we do as parents— how much we learn, how much we give of ourselves—there will never be guarantees.

Ultimately our teens are on their own journey down a winding river with rapids of all kinds, none of which we can control. But by offering connection, community, expectations, and accountability, we can rest with the confidence that they'll not only make it through, but even thrive. If the twelve-foot drops haven't shown up already, they are coming. But your teen will make it through, because they have you as their guide.

Epilogue:
The Final Chapter on
Adolescence

It's not uncommon for me to hear from former clients wanting to come back in for a tune-up or to deal with a new round of challenges. I got one such email a few years ago from Ben. He wrote, "Hi Yshai, I don't know if you remember me but you worked with me and my mom a while ago when I was in high school. I'm twenty-one now and I'm doing okay but wondering if I can come back in to see you."

Being a therapist is a weird job, because typically no news is good news. Clients don't typically come back to say hi and share all the ways they're flourishing. Of course, I let Ben know that I'd be happy to meet with him again.

I barely recognized him. At six foot one, he was almost as tall as me. He was muscular and sported a full beard! It had been five years since I last saw him, and I was eager to catch up.

Ben shared that he went away to college after high school but found it harder than he expected. He struggled socially and wasn't engaged academically. He ended up returning home after a lackluster fall term and has been living at home with his parents for the last two years. He had been working and taking a few classes at a local community college. He shared that he has been feeling a bit depressed (his state) and like a failure (his story).

Ben's mom, Jackie, reached out as well. She said she was worried about her son but mostly wanted guidance on how to support him at this stage of life. She had lots of questions. Now that he's twenty-one and living at home, should he be paying rent? Be expected to have a goal of moving out? Is it okay to have expectations around chores, curfews, or marijuana? Being twenty-one, Ben was certainly not a kid, but he wasn't ready to be a full card-carrying member of the adult community yet either.

Over the last few years, I've observed a noticeable trend of young adults and/or their parents reaching out to me. They're often looking for family therapy to help figure out this extended adolescence. I wouldn't go as far to say that twenty is the new fifteen, but young adulthood certainly looks different from the way it used to, and it's important that as parents we have realistic expectations for this stage of life.

As you now know from chapter 1, adolescence is a transition to adulthood. Unlike the start of adolescence, which has a clear marker of puberty, the end is defined culturally, and the path to it has gotten longer over time. It's now common for mature adulthood to begin around thirty.

This stage of life is an important part of adolescence, and because it's so long and distinct, it's useful for it to have its own name. The stage between approximately eighteen to thirty is now often referred to as emerging adulthood (EA). The term was coined by Jeffery Arnett, a researcher who has studied this period of life for decades.

The short version is, we're not done when our kids turn eighteen. Not at all. Stay with me.

Recall from chapter 2 that the PFC isn't done being remodeled until the mid-twenties. So, far from this delayed adulthood being a problem, I encourage you to view it as an opportunity. Arnett identified three phases that every young adult goes through during this period: launching, exploring, and landing.

Phase 1: Launching

This stage is what you might think. It typically follows completing high school. Launching often involves moving out of the house for the first time, whether that's going away to college or moving into an apartment or doing a gap year program. However, during this stage there's still a lot of returning home, along with emotional and financial reliance on parents.

Phase 2: Exploring

This is where the opportunity of EA lies, and it's the biggest change from previous generations. This phase is about discovering and learning from experiences. It's a process of practicing adulting, which might include being in a committed relationship, trying out a career path, and paying their own bills. When I talk to young people like Ben, or their parents, like Jackie, I want them to understand the value of taking advantage of this time in their life to learn and try new things. Yes, education is important, but it's often the less-interesting, grinding, or ill-fitting jobs that propel us toward something different and better. When it comes to relationships, the same can be said about getting your heart broken or breaking someone else's. These types of experiences often foster more reflection and fine-tune our partner and lifestyle preferences.

The period of exploring is a unique opportunity for young adults to define and deepen their sense of self and their values. A prolonged period of exploring will set your child up for a successful and fulfilling landing.

Phase 3: Landing

This is when they start to settle on a relationship, career, and lifestyle. They may be partnered, engaged, or married or own a house at this point. The hope is that the exploring they did set them up to land on a life trajectory that is fulfilling and a good match.

I share these stages with you only to help you get a better sense of where your young adult is at and what you can anticipate. These stages are highly variable. For example, some EA's may skip the exploring stage and go from launching to landing. This might look like finishing high school, getting their secondary education, getting married, and starting a family and career all by age twenty-two. Others explore for a very long time. Most of us know at least one person in their thirties, or even their forties, who still hasn't landed.

All This Means That Your Job Isn't Done

If you have a young adult in your family, you know this all too well. Your EA will continue to rely on you financially and emotionally. They'll ask you for money and to help bail them out of situations (not literally, I hope). They may make reckless choices at times. You can be all but assured that they'll make decisions that you don't agree with.

Your role will change in significant ways, but the importance of maintaining connection, expectations, and accountability will not. Your young adult still needs you. They need you to listen and care, particularly when they mess up, which they will.

They need you to maintain expectations and hold them accountable.

A young woman I worked with got a DUI while away at college. She was charged, had her license suspended, and was required to take a drug and alcohol class. Her parents showed love by visiting her on campus and taking her out to dinner. They practiced PACE. Their intention was to reassert their support, as she was understandably shaken and embarrassed. They also held her accountable by doing nothing to get her out of her jam. They validated how hard it would be without a car, and her having to take this extra class in addition to all her college classes would make for a challenging term. But they let her know they believed in her and that she could handle it.

I worked with this family throughout this process. I can't lie: I was a bit nervous and unsure about her outcome. But she did pull through and grew a lot from that stressful and embarrassing experience.

It's a Transition for You Too

EA is a transition for both of you. It's an opportunity to see your child as a free-thinking, interesting, thoughtful, and intelligent individual with their own hopes and dreams. Your EA will be much better at regulating than they were as a teen and may even be someone you occasionally rely on for coregulation.

The relationship between parent and child is often thought of as a vertical dynamic. We start out very top down. Over time this line should be tilting. Sometime during the EA stage the hope is that the line between the two of you becomes horizontal.

As you do your best to maintain PACE, expectations, and accountability, by the end of the exploring stage and beginning of landing, you'll hopefully get to experience a real and rich friendship with your child. One that includes mutual respect, shared vulnerability, support, and fun. EA is a time when your child will have the capacity to reflect a bit more on their childhood. Their mature PFC and vastly improved capacity to regulate make for lovely opportunities for reflection and healing with you.

To be clear, it can still be hard. You may continue to worry, and there will be occasional conflict. But my hope is that the work you've put in up to this point pays off in spades. That family and holiday get-togethers are not tension-filled obligations to get through but joyous occasions to look forward to.

I saw Ben off and on for several years through his mid-twenties. He had highs and lows, for sure. He struggled with the dilemma of wanting to save money while living at home while desperately wanting to move out and have more independence and autonomy. At one point he moved in with his girlfriend, until they broke up, forcing him to move back home. He graduated college at twenty-four and applied to law school, but soon after being accepted he realized that he didn't want to be a lawyer and was pursuing this only to make his dad (a successful lawyer) proud of him. On top of that, the thought of accumulating more college debt than he already had was something he just couldn't stomach. This is a very real concern that is impacting many EAs today. For a while after that, Ben explored and floundered.

Through our work together, I helped him get in touch with his own values and internal compass. He discovered that he enjoyed cooking, and he got a job as a cook in a restaurant. It was intense at times, but he had never been happier. I know his parents were worried about him, so with Ben's permission I had a couple of sessions with them to help them get perspective.

Meeting with Ben's Parents

Ben was afraid that his parents would be disappointed in him and his life decisions, so I was curious to see for myself what they were thinking. As is often the case, Ben's anxiety about letting down his parents was unfounded. They acknowledged that yes, they did worry about him sometimes, but they also noticed that he'd seemed happier since breaking up with his girlfriend and getting this new job as a cook. His dad stated that he wasn't disappointed at all about Ben's not going to law school.

Mostly his parents were confused. They just wanted to be supportive but didn't know how. Since they'd both graduated college at twenty-two and started grad school and their careers right afterward, they couldn't relate to Ben's path.

Here's the advice I offered his parents that I hope you find helpful with your EA as well.

- *Don't compare your experiences during this time with your child's.* The environment, culture, and expectations are much different for this generation. It's not uncommon to graduate late and meander before settling on a career at thirty.

- *Look for movement and maturation.* As long as your EA is trying new things, engaged with their community and other people, they're likely doing well. It's concerning only if they are stagnant, not leaving the house, languishing without work or school, isolated, or using drugs or alcohol to excess.

- *Appreciate the opportunity for a new kind of relationship.* You can expect them to have much more capacity for fun and thoughtful conversations. Start building a relationship that gradually takes you out of the parental role. This will be harder than it sounds, because your EA may have a hard time acting like an adult around you, still expecting you to talk to and treat them like a child. You can help change that pattern by letting them fail and make their own decisions.

Parenting doesn't just stop, but it changes a lot. As your teen becomes an EA, they will still need you and rely on you for a while. They may still stress you out. At the same time, the combination of their mature PFC and life experiences will make them much easier to talk to and more fun to spend time with.

Whether we're guiding our children through phase 1, 2, or EA, parenting will constitute the bulk of our lifespan. There will always be ups and downs with no guarantees. Whatever the circumstances you find yourself in with your teen or EA, remember what really matters: authentic connection, expectations, and accountability. When you get distracted by their wonky choices and lapses, come back to those three things, and a renewed path forward will reveal itself.

Acknowledgments

I've always loved books, particularly nonfiction books, but I never thought of myself as a writer or the kind of person who could write a book. The biggest hurdle I had to overcome was fear. It took the support, encouragement, and feedback of a lot of people to help me overcome that and get this book out in the world.

I'm honored and lucky to get to make a living doing what I love and helping people along the way. I've learned something from every teenager, parent, and family that I've ever had the privilege of working with or meeting at a workshop or webinar. This book couldn't have happened without your courage and vulnerability.

I'm extremely grateful to my consult group: Lynn, Ally, Erica, Debbie, and Mariah. You guys are so smart and supportive. You challenge and sharpen my thinking and have helped make this book what it is. Howard Hiton, thank you for your feedback and support with this manuscript. Your mentorship and support over the years has meant a lot to me.

This book rests on the shoulders of some brilliant and creative thinkers. Thank you, Daniel Hughes, for your input and support on the PACE chapter. Your work and writing have inspired me for many years. I'm immensely appreciative of the groundbreaking work of Stephen Porges and Deb Dana, which laid the foundation for this book. Throughout my career as an adolescent therapist, there isn't one individual who's influenced my work more than Laurence Steinberg, whose research and thinking heavily influenced these pages.

I truly don't know if this book would have gotten published without the support of my first editor, Meghan Hill. Meghan, I hired you as an editor with very little confidence in my ability to write something worthy of being published. I simply thought you would provide editing. But you did much more than that: You helped me believe that I had something here that was unique and solid and could help a lot of parents. I'll always be grateful to you.

Rachel Hershenberg, thank you for the introduction to Ryan Buresh at New Harbinger. Ryan, your ongoing and steady support to me as a first-time writer was so helpful. I truly appreciated and enjoyed the relationship we developed through the process of getting this book out. I'm grateful to an amazing editing team: Jennifer Holder, Callie Brown, and Kristi Hein. Your honesty and insights took this manuscript to new levels. Lastly, there were a lot of people at NH working hard behind the scenes to get this book out into the world, from designing an amazing cover to publicity and marketing. Thank you!

Now for the personal.

James, thank you for letting me share a glimpse of your story with the world. You have come so far. You're a success story, and I'm so grateful that we've remained close over these years.

I grew up in a two-bedroom apartment with my mom, who always maintained bookshelves filled to the brim with self-help and nonfiction books. Thanks, Mom, for this early exposure. Who would have thought I'd one day be the author of a book that's sitting on one of your bookshelves?

To my dad, for always being involved and engaged in my life, both growing up and as an adult. I forgive you for grounding me that weekend. Lynne, thanks for keeping him in check and always being there for us as well. The countless hours spent working on this book were much easier knowing we could count on you to help with childcare or anything else we needed.

I'm extremely lucky to have a close-knit family in Portland. My kids really do have a village. To Rachel and Han, thank you for your support and for being secondary parents to our kids. Soo, Lacey, Ben, Gwen, Steve,

Carol: Our kids adore you (we do too), and we are so grateful for your enduring support and love.

To my men's circle: Thanks for being such a supportive group of friends and for offering your encouragement, and jokes, every step of the way.

Thank you, Lisa, for being such a phenomenal therapist and helping Mariah and me navigate the inevitable ups and downs of marriage and life.

Finally, Mariah, I can't imagine being married to a better human being or parent to our kids. You do so much for our family and truly walk the talk of this book. I learn so much from the way you show up with our kids. Thank you for all the time you spent editing and helping me improve this manuscript. You've been my biggest fan and cheerleader throughout this process, and it's meant more than you know. I love you.

Endnotes

1   American Academy of Pediatrics (AAP), the American Academy of Child and Adolescent Psychiatry (AACAP), and the Children's Hospital Association (CHA), "Pediatricians, Child and Adolescent Psychiatrists and Children's Hospitals Declare National Emergency in Children's Mental Health," October 19, 2021, https://www.aap.org /en/news-room/news-releases/aap/2021/pediatricians-child-and -adolescent-psychiatrists-and-childrens-hospitals-declare-national -emergency-for-childrens-mental-health.

2   Matt Richtel, "The Surgeon General's New Mission: Adolescent Mental Health," *New York Times*, March 21, 2023.

3   Laurence Steinberg and Wendy Steinberg, *Crossing Paths: How Your Child's Adolescence Triggers Your Own Crisis* (Simon & Schuster, 1994).

4   Laurence Steinberg, *Age of Opportunity: Lessons from the New Science of Adolescence* (HarperCollins, 2014).

5   Destin Sandlin, "The Backwards Brain Bicycle," *Smarter Every Day*, https://www.youtube.com/watch?v=MFzDaBzBlL0&t=33s.

6   Todd A. Hare, Nim Tottenham, Adriana Galvan, Henning U. Voss, Gary H. Glover, and B. J. Casey, "Biological Substrates of Emotional Reactivity and Regulation in Adolescence During an Emotional Go-Nogo Task," *Biological Psychiatry* 63, no. 10 (May 2008): 927–934, https://doi.org/10.1016/j.biopsych.2008.03.015.

7   Stephen Porges, *The Polyvagal Theory: Neurophysiological Foundations of Emotions, Attachment, Communication, and Self-regulation* (Norton, 2011).

8   Deb Dana, *The Polyvagal Theory in Therapy: Engaging the Rhythm of Regulation* (Norton, 2018); *Anchored: How to Befriend Your Nervous System Using Polyvagal Theory* (Sounds True, 2021); *Polyvagal Practices: Anchoring the Self in Safety* (Norton, 2023).

9   A. N. Cooke and A. G. Halberstadt, "Adultification, Anger Bias, and Adults' Different Perceptions of Black and White Children," *Cognition and Emotion* 35, no. 7 (2021): 1416–22.

10   Bruce Perry and Oprah Winfrey, *What Happened to You? Conversations on Trauma, Resilience, and Healing* (Flatiron Books, 2021).

11   Harvard Health Publishing, "Can Relationships Boost Longevity and Well-being?" June 1, 2017, https://www.health.harvard.edu /mental-health/can-relationships-boost-longevity-and-well-being.

12   Robert W. Blum and Peggy Ann Rinehart, "Reducing the Risk: Connections That Make a Difference in the Lives of Youth," *Youth Studies Australia* 16, no. 4 (December 1997): 37–50.

13   Albert Mehrabian and Morton Wiener, "Decoding of Inconsistent Communications," *Journal of Personality and Social Psychology* 6, no. 1 (1997): 109–114.

14   Barbara L. Fredrickson, *Positivity: Top-notch Research Reveals the 3 to 1 Ratio That Will Change Your Life* (Crown Publishing Group, 2009).

15   James A. Coan, Hillary S. Schaefer, and Richard J. Davidson, "Lending a Hand: Social Regulation of the Neural Response to Threat," *Psychological Science* 17, no. 12 (2006): 1032–1039.

16   Michael W Kraus, Cassey Huang, and Dacher Keltner, "Tactile Communication, Cooperation, and Performance: An Ethological Study of the NBA," *Emotion* 10, no. 6 (2010): 745–749.

17   Daniel Hughes, *Attachment-Focused Family Therapy* (Norton, 2007), 68.

18   Daniel Hughes and Jonathan Baylin, *Brain-Based Parenting: The Neuroscience of Caregiving for Healthy Attachment* (Norton, 2012).

19   Sergio M. Pellis, Vivien C. Pellis, and Heather C. Bell, "The Function of Play in the Development of the Social Brain," *American Journal of Play* 2, no. 3 (2010): 278–296.

20   Tara Brach, *Radical Acceptance: Embracing Your Life with the Heart of a Buddha* (Bantam Books, 2003).

21   "The Unwanted Party Guest: An Acceptance & Commitment Therapy (ACT) Metaphor," https://www.youtube.com/watch?v =VYht-guymF4.

22   Hughes, *Attachment-Focused Family Therapy* (n. 17).

23   Joseph P. Allen, Joanna Chango, David Szwedo, Megan Schad, and Emily Marston, "Predictors of Susceptibility to Peer Influence Regarding Substance Use in Adolescence," *Child Development* 83, no. 1 (2012): 337–350.

24   Elly Brett, "New BHF Report Finds Young People Are More Interested in Volunteering Than Older Generations," British Heart Foundation (September 16, 2019), https://www.bhf.org.uk /what-we-do/news-from-the-bhf/news-archive/2019/september/new -bhf-report-finds-young-people-are-more-interested-in-volunteering -than-older-generations.

25   Juliana Menasce Horowitz and Nikki Graf, "Most U.S. Teens See Anxiety and Depression as a Major Problem Among Their Peers," Pew Research Center, February 20, 2019, https://www.pewresearch .org/social-trends/2019/02/20/most-u-s-teens-see-anxiety-and -depression-as-a-major-problem-among-their-peers.

26 Margo Gardner and Laurence Steinberg, "Peer Influence on Risk Taking, Risk Preference, and Risky Decision Making in Adolescence and Adulthood: An Experimental Study," *Developmental Psychology* 41, no. 4 (2005): 625–635, https://doi.org/10.1037/0012-1649.41.4.625.

27 Lisa Damour, *The Emotional Lives of Teenagers: Raising Connected, Capable, and Compassionate Adolescents* (Ballantine Books, 2023).

28 Peggy Orenstein, "Will We Ever Figure Out How to Talk to Boys About Sex?" *New York Times*, January 10, 2020, https://www.nytimes.com/2020/01/10/opinion/sunday/boys-sex.html.

29 Michael B. Robb and Supreet Mann, *Teens and Pornography* (Common Sense, 2023), https://www.commonsensemedia.org/sites/default/files/research/report/2022-teens-and-pornography-final-web.pdf.

30 Jessica Boyer, "New Name, Same Harm," *Guttmacher Policy Review*, February 28, 2018, https://www.guttmacher.org/gpr/2018/02/new-name-same-harm-rebranding-federal-abstinence-only-programs; Andrea Zelinski, "Rewrite of Texas Sex Education Standards Could Include Lessons on Contraception, Gender Identity," *Houston Chronicle*, June 13, 2019, https://www.expressnews.com/news/education/article/Rewrite-of-Texas-sex-education-standards-could-13990827.php; Advocates for Youth, "Sexual Education: Research and Results," Fact Sheet, Washington, DC: Advocates for Youth (2009), https://advocatesforyouth.org/wp-content/uploads/storage//advfy/documents/school-health-equity/sexual-healthed-research-and-results.pdf.

31 Patricia Goodson, Eric R. Buhi, and Sarah C. Dunsmore, "Self-esteem and Adolescent Sexual Behaviors, Attitudes, and Intentions: A Systematic Review," *Journal of Adolescent Health* 38, no. 3 (2006): 310–19, https://doi.org/10.1016/j.jadohealth.2005.05.026.

32 Hiltrud Otto and Heidi Keller (Eds.), *Different Faces of Attachment: Cultural Variations on a Universal Human Need* (Cambridge University Press, 2014).

33 W. Andrews Collins and Laurence Steinberg, "Adolescent Development in Interpersonal Context," in *Handbook of Child Psychology: Social, Emotional, and Personality Development*, ed. William Damon, Richard M. Lerner, and Nancy Eisenberg (Wiley, 2006), 1003–1067.

34 Perry and Winfrey, *What Happened to You?* (n. 10).

35 Diana Divecha, "All Families Have Conflict. Here's How to Repair It," *Yes!* (December 25, 2020), https://www.yesmagazine.org /opinion/2020/12/25/family-conflict-repair.

Yshai Boussi, LPC, is a licensed professional counselor who has helped teens, young adults, and families for more than twenty years. He runs a private practice with his wife Mariah—in Portland, OR—called Portland Family Counseling, and is a parent and foster parent. Yshai is a highly sought-after speaker, and writes a parenting blog on his website: www. yshaiboussi.com.

Real change *is* possible

For more than forty-five years, New Harbinger has published proven-effective self-help books and pioneering workbooks to help readers of all ages and backgrounds improve mental health and well-being, and achieve lasting personal growth. In addition, our spirituality books offer profound guidance for deepening awareness and cultivating healing, self-discovery, and fulfillment.

Founded by psychologist Matthew McKay and Patrick Fanning, New Harbinger is proud to be an independent, employee-owned company. Our books reflect our core values of integrity, innovation, commitment, sustainability, compassion, and trust. Written by leaders in the field and recommended by therapists worldwide, New Harbinger books are practical, accessible, and provide real tools for real change.

newharbingerpublications